KARMA'S A WITCH

KARMA'S
A WITCH

Midia Star

GODSFIELD

First published in Great Britain in 2025 by Godsfield Press,
an imprint of Octopus Publishing Group Ltd
Carmelite House, 50 Victoria Embankment
London EC4Y 0DZ
www.octopusbooks.co.uk

An Hachette UK Company
www.hachette.co.uk

The authorized representative in the EEA is Hachette Ireland,
8 Castlecourt Centre, Dublin 15, D15 XTP3, Ireland (email: info@hbgi.ie)

Text copyright © Midia Star 2025
Illustrations copyright © Octopus Publishing Group 2025

Distributed in the US by Hachette Book Group
1290 Avenue of the Americas, 4th and 5th Floors
New York, NY 10104

Distributed in Canada by Canadian Manda Group
664 Annette St., Toronto, Ontario, Canada M6S 2C8

ISBN 978 1 84181 607 4

A CIP catalogue record for this book is available from the British Library.

Printed and bound in China.
10 9 8 7 6 5 4 3 2 1

Commissioning Editor: Louisa Johnson
Copy Editor: Tara O'Sullivan
Art Director: Yasia Williams
Illustrator: Natalie Muir
Production Manager: Caroline Alberti

contents

PART ONE:
introduction

WHat is KaRMa?

Karma (noun): 'The sum of a person's actions in this and previous states of existence, viewed as deciding their fate in future existences.'

Karma – it's a bit misunderstood, really.

When we say things like, 'Don't worry, karma will catch up with them,' or, 'That's karma for you!' we think of it in terms of vengeance, but karma is so much more than that.

Karma is a Sanskrit word, originally adopted by both Hindu and Buddhist philosophies to explain how a person's behaviour will eventually play a part in their future. In every philosophy and religion, you will find a reference to karma. The Bible states: 'Whoever sows injustice reaps calamity, and the rod they wield in fury will be broken' (Proverbs 22:8), while the Buddhist faith says that our past deeds will repay us now and forever. In Hinduism, it is believed that karma not only affects our current life, but our past and future lives, too.

The modern attitude towards karma tends to be less concerned with what might happen to our souls when we die, and more focused on the consequences that may be experienced by those who set out to cause harm to others. We've all heard the expression 'Karma's a b*tch', which means that what we send out will eventually return to us. Basically, karma is, and always has been, a law of cause and effect.

Karma has always played a large role in witchcraft. Many don't understand how karma and magic work (see 'Witchy Misconceptions', page 10). It's not like the movies where you pluck a hair from someone who has wronged you and they burn in hell. Karma magic is much more subtle than that. It's all about consequences, justice, fairness and protecting yourself, rather than setting out to destroy your enemies (don't worry, they will do that themselves).

Karma is less about setting wrongs right, and more about protecting your inner peace, self-worth and self-confidence. It's amazing how quickly another person's energy can have a huge effect on us and turn us into someone we hardly recognize.

It is said that everyone gets the life they deserve. And believe me, karma – mixed with a little magic – always makes sure that happens.

HOW TO USE THIS BOOK

In this book, you will discover the transformative power of karma magic and, more importantly, how to craft your own spells to shield yourself from the people who are trying to harm you in some way. Whether it's an ex who just won't leave you alone, a boss who takes the credit for your work, a social-media troll who keeps hassling you, a neighbour who is less than neighbourly, or a jealous, back-stabbing friend-turned-enemy, this book covers all modern situations. Remember: this is not about getting your own back; it's about protecting your peace by giving karma a little nudge in the right direction.

Part One of this book is dedicated to some basic witchy info. Together, we will learn a bit about the history of witchcraft and karma magic, clear up some misconceptions, discover the right tools for spellwork, unlock the power of goddesses and lunar cycles, and learn how to grow the best herbs so that you have everything you need on hand for your spells.

Part Two takes you through over 60 easy spells you can refer to again and again to ensure that you are protected from the harm of others. There is no need to worry about subtlety, tact and anonymity; these spells can all be conducted in a gentle, understated way that will leave your perpetrator scratching their head in confusion.

Each spell has been designed so that you can perform it even with no prior experience or knowledge of witchcraft. That being said, I strongly encourage you to read Part One first, as the spells may make more sense if you do. And, as they say, knowledge is power!

My hope is that you never feel alone again once you learn about the craft of spellcasting. After reading this book, you will feel the universe helping you and your confidence will grow. You will know that you are in charge of your own life, and so you will never feel dependent on anyone else again. How far you delve into the subject is up to you, but from my own personal experience, once you discover how powerful you can be, you will never feel fear again.

witchy misconceptions

In witchcraft, we believe that all actions and intentions have consequences. If your life choices come from a place of care, joy or compassion, you will experience a positive outcome. However, if they are derived from a place of anger, fear or spite, you will experience a negative outcome.

There are a lot of misconceptions surrounding witchcraft, witches and karma, so let's clear up a few of these before we begin ...

'WHEN SOMEONE DOES SOMETHING HATEFUL AGAINST ANOTHER PERSON, THREE BAD THINGS HAPPEN TO THEM IN RETURN.'

In witchcraft and Wicca, karma is often called the Threefold Law, or sometimes the Rule of Three. Some people who practise witchcraft believe that our actions and intentions have vibrational consequences, which are returned to us three times over. Some witches even believe that they are returned to us ten times.

Now, this is where it gets interesting – because many will argue that if there was such a thing as karma, then why are awful people still wandering around among us and not suffering as they should be? Well, karma is not quite as simple as that. It doesn't automatically punish someone for their bad deeds, so if you're hoping that your cheating ex will get struck by lightning three times, then think again. People don't necessarily get what we think they deserve, which is why there are many lying, evil and cheating people still walking the earth.

What does happen, though, is that the universe matches their vibrations.

No number of pins in an effigy of your cheating ex-partner is going to make them change their ways. Nor will this cause them actual physical pain. What will happen, however, is that they will continue to go through life cheating on their future partners, and as a result they will never be able to settle down or find peace with just one person. They will always be searching for love and happiness, and they will never find it. Alternatively, they may fall madly in love with someone who does the same to them. This is their karma. It's all about the vibrations they are putting out into the world and the repercussions that will follow for them.

People who practise witchcraft know that whatever energy you put out into the world is kind of like a boomerang; it will come back to you. If you are constantly negative and miserable, then your life will be consistently full of negative and miserable happenings. Someone who is set on hurting others will eventually suffer as a consequence of their actions, but this may not happen as we envisage – and it may not specifically happen three times.

The misconception surrounding the Threefold Law is believed to have originated from a chap called Gerald Garner. Garner was one of the first influential figures in the development of the Wiccan religion. However, he was also a fiction writer, and he used the definition of the Threefold Law in his fictional writings about witchcraft. So, the Threefold Law is more to do with fiction

than fact – although many witches consider it to be a true law and interpret it literally, perhaps because the number three does tend to have mysterious and esoteric properties in history, culture and religion. For example, in Greek mythology there were three Fates who controlled the destinies of mortal humans, while in Christianity, we see the trinity of Father, Son and Holy Spirit.

The truth is that the whole concept of the Threefold Law is not about how many times a person's good or bad actions will return to them; it could be 10 times, 50 or even more. What it's really about is tapping in to the energy, vibrations and intention of a person who is making life difficult for you in some way and returning this energy to them. Doing this is less about punishing them directly than protecting yourself from further harm.

While someone who has harmed you will eventually reap what they've sown, when you apply a little karma magic, you tend to accelerate the process. By utilizing magic, you can take back your power so that no one can harm you again.

'YOU CAN SPOT A WITCH A MILE AWAY, WITH THEIR LONG BLACK HAIR, HEAVY EYELINER AND PENTAGRAM HANGING FROM THEIR NECK!'

...No! While I love a bit of black eyeliner, I do not have long black hair, nor do I wear a pentagram. The only clue that I practise and believe in the Craft is the cauldron in my home. You may see witches on social media dressed up in robes and hats, but most people who practise witchcraft look just like any other human being. The witch in your life could be the woman at the checkout who just served you, or that one neighbour who drives the red Mini and works for the council, or that bloke who mows the cricket pitch in the summer. Anyone can be a witch, and you wouldn't know it. While some witches like to advertise the fact that they practise the Craft, there are just as many who prefer to remain anonymous. It's a bit like trying to spot someone who practises Christianity or Buddhism: unless they wear something declaring their chosen faith, you simply would never know.

'WITCHES ARE EVIL AND WORSHIP THE DEVIL!'

While novels and movies might suggest otherwise, people who practise witchcraft are some of the most gentle, authentic, loving and peaceful human beings in the world. Wicca is a faith of love, light and positive blessings. Anyone who tells you that witches are evil and summon dark forces hasn't been educated about what the faith is really about. Many are ignorant about witchcraft and it's easy to fear something we don't understand. When we're unwilling to research a subject, it's easier to believe the stories handed down to us. People who practise witchcraft are all about protecting animals, nature and our fellow humans. Those people who advertise that they can hex your ex or put a curse on someone for you may be many other things, but witches they are not.

'WITCHES ARE DE-LU-LU!'

That is, until someone wants a Tarot reading or requests a spell to make someone fall in love with them! Witchcraft is not a faith that is set in stone, and the people who are attracted to this faith are pioneers who know that there is more to life than meets the eye. This is why witches have always been labelled as odd or delusional. This is also the reason why most witches keep their beliefs quiet and don't go around advertising their magic. If you'd called yourself a witch 300 years ago, you'd have had a torch-wielding mob outside your front door. Sadly, that's a common reaction in society: when people don't understand or are fearful of someone, they deem them delusional or odd. They reject them or persecute them. So, no, witches are far from de-lu-lu. In fact, they are some of the most intuitive and kindest people you will ever meet.

'WITCHES WILL CURSE YOU IF YOU UPSET THEM!'

Real witches are peace-loving people who believe in equality and justice across the board. We do not go round intentionally harming others, even if we have been harmed ourselves. This is because we believe heavily in the power of karma. We may tap in to our own personal power to help give karma a little nudge in the right direction, but as I mentioned at the beginning of this book, the intention is all about protecting yourself, rather than casting bad luck upon someone else.

That being said, I have discovered that when I do cast spells to protect myself from harm and hate from someone, something bad invariably does happen to the perpetrator. Again, this is the whole concept of the Craft – you use it to protect yourself. Whatever happens to someone who harms or hates on you is their own doing, not yours.

'WITCH COVENS ARE CULTS.'

A coven is simply a group of people with a shared interest in witchcraft who gather to swap spells, stories and herbal remedies, and to learn from those more experienced. It's no different to a book-club meeting or a coffee catch-up with a few like-minded friends. The idea that covens meet in secret, under the cloak of darkness, is a leftover belief from darker times when those labelled as witches were persecuted. Modern coven members do not gather naked in the woods under the full moon to perform rituals and sacrifice small children, as some movies would lead you to believe. More often, members will meet at one another's houses in the suburbs and bring cake. Given that there is still a stigma associated with witches and witchcraft, covens do not go door to door recruiting members to join them, and they certainly wouldn't be wanting just anyone to join. Also, there are many witches, like me, who do not belong to a coven – we are known as 'solitary' or 'hedge witches'.

'WITCHES MAKE POISONOUS POTIONS.'

In Shakespeare's *Macbeth*, we see the three witches sing:

DOUBLE, DOUBLE TOIL AND TROUBLE;
FIRE BURN AND CALDRON BUBBLE.
FILLET OF A FENNY SNAKE
IN THE CALDRON BOIL AND BAKE;
EYE OF NEWT AND TOE OF FROG,
WOOL OF BAT AND TONGUE OF DOG ...

This little rhyme has aided the misconception that witches sit around crafting poisonous potions and toxic tonics that they then dispense to unwitting victims. What most people don't know is that these ingredients are actually the alternative names for various healing plants, flowers and seeds. It's thought that 'eye of newt' most likely refers to wild mustard seed, for example.

It's believed that the word 'witch' came from Germany and represented those who had almost mystical powers that could not be explained by logical means. Before this word became popularized and stigmatized, every village would have had a 'wise woman'. This woman would appear to be all-knowing and would supply her neighbours with cures for their aliments – a medieval pharmacist, if you like. She would have studied herbal remedies, and would have been able to mix potions and lotions that could treat everything from eczema to smallpox. She would also have been the local midwife. She would never have harmed another – and no modern witch should, either.

'WITCHES CAN FLY.'

With EasyJet, maybe. But no, there is no truth in a witch's ability to fly, either by themselves, on a broomstick or using any other object. The myth that witches can fly on broomsticks possibly originated in the effects that some herbs and plants had on people when ingested. For example, plants such as mandrake root have hallucinogenic effects that can make a person feel like they are floating in the air. Broomsticks do serve a real function for witches, however (see page 18).

'WITCHES ALWAYS HAVE A BLACK CAT.'

While most witches adore all animals and creatures, not all have a cat, black or otherwise. I have six dogs, and I've never owned a cat in my life. Many witches have animal pets, which they refer to as familiars. A familiar is an animal that they feel a spiritual connection with and will be their guardian and protector for life. While many witches do choose cats as their familiars, others have dogs, birds, rabbits, horses or lizards. Fiction and movies often depict familiars as being able to shape-shift, but this is another misconception.

witchy tools

While tools such as an altar, herbs, crystals and candles are all very lovely to have and can definitely help enhance the power of your spells, it's important to remember that they are all just tools. The most important tool you will ever need is YOU!

It's useful to remember that historically, witches used certain tools because they had to. For example, because there was no electricity, everyone would use candles to light their homes, and so candles soon became a big part of witchy rituals. And owning a cauldron wasn't necessarily a sign that someone was a witch. Every home used to have one; they were essentially huge cooking pots made from cast iron.

So, you can use as many tools as you wish to perform spells and magic, but it is not a necessity. The most important tool is your intention. I've known many witches who use no ingredients or tools and simply focus on what they want to manifest through thought and meditation, and they do this very successfully. However, if you want to embrace the whole witchy experience, below are some tools that will help you feel more connected to the power of the universe.

Remember that witchcraft should be about whatever you want it to be about. You don't necessarily have to know and remember all the sabbats throughout the year, nor should you always carry a particular crystal around with you. If you failed to leave an offering to your ancestors when you cast a spell, or forgot to charge your cards or crystals on the last full moon – it's OK!

Witchcraft and spellcasting are a very personal thing, and there are no exact rights and wrongs. What you have read and will continue to read about witchcraft generally comes from generations of people who have honed their Craft and have passed that information on. It in no way means that this way of doing things is set in stone, nor does it mean that it's how it should be done. All it means is that it worked for that particular person, but it might not work that way for you. It annoys me greatly when certain people who practise witchcraft attack other witches by saying their methods are incorrect. This attitude throws witchcraft into the realms of organized religion. Witchcraft was never intended to be about rules and regulations. It is whatever you want it to be.

We all lead very busy lives these days. The best witches are imperfect witches, and, over time, you will discover your own style, so please don't stress if you don't have a particular ingredient, or you can't wait until the next full moon. Your magic will be just as powerful as any other witch because, at the end of the day, what it boils down to is your intention.

Candles

Candles originated over 5,000 years ago when ancient Egyptians used reeds and animal fats to illuminate their surroundings. Since then, people have used candles for everything from emergency lighting to celebrating birthdays, remembering loved ones that have passed, and filling their homes with fragrance – and, of course, they help us to enhance our spells.

Witches use candles more than any other tool when spellcasting because they are believed to be the closest thing to the element of fire, which gives more power to a spell. Additionally, candle spells require very little equipment (often just a candle, a match and your intention), and so they are some of the easiest to perform.

You can make your candle spells more powerful by engraving your candle with a silver pin, anointing them with oil, and burning herb bundles, but often the simplest spells are the most powerful spells. I know many witches who buy packets of birthday cake candles because they are much cheaper than pillar candles.

CANDLE COLOURS

When colour started being added to wax, witches soon discovered that different colours could enhance the spells and deliver faster results. Below are the most powerful colours and the spells they work best for:

Red: Red candles work best for love, action and vitality, and for karma to be returned.

Orange: Orange candles work best for peace, self-confidence and success.

Yellow: Yellow candles work best for communication and manifestation, and for spells of urgency.

Green: Green candles work best for money, prosperity and luck.

Purple: Purple candles work best to increase psychic powers and healing.

Black: Black candles work best for banishing negativity, hexing and protection.

White: White candles work best for healing and purity, although spells tend to have less intensity.

Again, you do not need to invest in a whole load of candles, but they have been shown to speed up your spells. You can use fragranced candles, if you prefer.

A BROOM

It is believed that the first images of witches and brooms date back to 1451 as illustrations for a poem written by Martin Le Franc. The image shows a woman flying through the air on a broom. The idea that witches could fly on brooms was an urban myth made up to increase fear of people who practised witchcraft.

The real reason witches would have a broom is much more practical. There were no carpets or modern heating in homes, so the only means of heat would have been an open fire. This would create dust and ash. As there was no mass production of cleaning materials, women would make their own brooms out of natural products – twigs, branches and twine. However, witches believed that their natural brooms held magical properties, and they would use them to ward off evil from entering their surroundings by firstly sweeping out any negative energy a visitor might bring into the home, and then placing the broom bristles-side up, so as to ward off any negative energy returning.

Over time, brooms became connected with celebrations and superstitions. Newlyweds would jump the broom to ensure a happy and healthy marriage, and farmers would dance with brooms and pitchforks under the light of a full moon to encourage a healthy crop for the following year.

Today, witches use brooms in much the same way – to ward off evil or negativity, to celebrate the changing of the seasons and to banish any bad energy from the home. Although you can now buy witch's broomsticks from the internet, it's really fun to make your own and it gives the broom more power because it is personal to you.

SOME BROOMSTICK FOLKLORE

- Never sweep at night, or you might wake the spirits from their slumber.

- Stand the broom, bristles up, by the front door to ward off evil and bring good luck instead.

- Raise a storm by shaking a wet broom over your head.

- Never take an old broom into a new home – make a new one if you move house.

- Jump over the boom nine times and you will be married within one year.

- Lay a broom under your bed for protection.

How to make your own broomstick

Source and collect your materials.
Traditionally, the bristles of a witch's broomstick would have been made from hawthorn. The hawthorn has tiny little spikes on its branches, which are believed to spike any negativity and stop it from entering the home. Hawthorn can be found in most areas of the countryside in the form of roadside bushes, but make sure you take a pair of gloves with you because of those prickles! Alternatively, you can use any woody plant. Some witches prefer a softer broom and will make theirs out of hay, but hay brooms can easily lose their bristles over time, so I would suggest a more robust material, such as hawthorn, willow or forsythia. Many witches like to include flowers such as lavender and heather or berries in their brooms. You will also need to find a long branch to act as the handle.

Assemble your broom.
Lay your materials on the floor and gather all the twigs and flowers together around the handle. With ordinary garden twine, carefully wrap the branches around the broom handle. You may need someone else to help you with this part, as it can be quite tricky to do it on your own.

Repeat until your broom head is full and bushy. It pays to wrap the twine around the handle many times, and you can secure it further with some hot glue if you wish. The last thing you want is for it to fall apart when you're brushing away any negativity.

Add your finishing touches.
Once you're happy with your broom and it's tied securely, you can add some personal touches such as glitter, charms or colourful ribbon to the handle.

Bless your broom.
Mix one teaspoon of household salt into a spray bottle of water and spray the broom all over, saying:

Blessed is this besom with protection and positivity, so mote it be.

Leave it to dry and then use it to swish any negative energy out of your home.

A Book of Shadows

A Book of Shadows is basically a notebook to hold all your spells, lists of herbs and ingredients, and anything else related to spellcasting. Don't be fooled into thinking that you have to have a leatherbound grimoire that's been blessed by a thousand goddesses – you don't. The Books of Shadows that are depicted in movies, leatherbound and covered in dust and cobwebs, are no more magical than a notebook from your local stationery store. It is a personal preference, of course, and if you feel that you would prefer a more traditional style of book, by all means, buy one.

There are just two things I would suggest: the first is that you choose a book with a hard cover, because the more experienced you become in spellcasting, the more you will need to write in your Book of Shadows, and over time it will become worn. The second is that you choose a notebook with a lot of pages, because otherwise you will have filled it up before you know it and will have several books to refer to rather than just one big one.

You can put whatever you feel like in your Book of Shadows – this could be spells, pressed flowers, herbs or leaves you find useful, information about the moon phases, notes on how long a spell took to manifest, Tarot readings, etc. Some witches like to include pockets in their Book of Shadows to hold and protect their dried herbs.

Most witches will write in their Book of Shadows by hand, and I feel this is something that helps us to connect with Wicca. There's something nice about taking a few minutes away from the modern world to sit and write in a notebook. Some modern witches do prefer to have an electronic file on their computer/phone/device as their Book of Shadows, but I prefer to use something more tangible that you can refer to as the years go by and you learn more about your Craft.

If you decide to make a Book of Shadows, be sure to use it only for your magic work and nothing else, otherwise it will become just another notebook rather than a place devoted to recording your spellwork.

CRYSTALS

Because crystals are natural products that have mystical properties, they are often used in spells. Witches believe that crystal energy helps them to focus, so that their intentional energy is sent in the right direction rather than being scattered around, which is particularly important in karma spells.

Visit any alternative gift shop and you'll see an array of crystals on display. You can even buy candles infused with crystals now, giving you the benefit of both crystal and candle in one go for optimal power.

You will often see what are known as crystal wands, which are long sticks of crystals such as clear quartz. Clear quartz is perfect for karma spells because it promotes healing, repels negative energy, and gives optimism and peace – all essential for this kind of spellwork. You can tell if a quartz crystal is real by holding it up to the light. If it's real, you will be able to see the light through it and objects will look slightly distorted.

While there are many schools of thought as to which crystal you should use for a specific spell, I always advise going with your instincts when choosing crystals. Some will repel you, whereas others will feel 'right'. It really is a personal thing, and no two witches will be drawn to the same crystal.

Real crystals should feel cool to the touch when you pick them up, and if you close your hand around one, it will warm up in your hand.

This is how you can tell if you have a real or a fake crystal. Fake crystals will be the same temperature as the room, and you won't feel anything when you pick them up, neither will they warm up in your hand.

Crystals are natural energy amplifiers and will absorb and store energy, so it's important to cleanse them by washing them in water when you've finished using them in a spell.

An altar

Some witches choose to have an altar where they keep all their witchery tools, ready to cast a spell or two. An altar is basically a special place where you can practise your Craft in peace.

It is not a necessary requirement to have your witchcraft items on display, however, and many witches don't feel comfortable with other people in their home knowing about their spellworking area for fear of ridicule. This is perfectly understandable, and if you don't want anyone to know that you practise witchcraft, you can store anything witchy in a shoebox under the bed. Don't feel you have to announce it to the world if you're not comfortable.

A witch's altar is personal to the individual. Some witches like to dedicate a whole room to their Craft, others have a small coffee table in their living room or bedroom.

Many witches make sure that their altars face north because north is associated with the earth element, but again, this is just a personal preference.

As to what you put on your altar, that is entirely up to you, but most witches will have candles, salt, an athame (a witch's knife), a wand, Tarot/oracle cards, various herbs, a pentagram symbol and sometimes an ornament or two of their favourite deities or goddesses.

A wand

We're all familiar with the association between witches, wizards and wands from modern books and movies, but wands can actually be dated back to the ancient Egyptians. It is believed they would use wands in ceremonial magic rituals as they were seen as a tool of power. The term 'wand' was also used as a measurement within the British Isles.

In modern witchcraft, the wand represents the direction of energy when casting a spell. Witches will also use a wand to activate the energy from their crystals, draw circles of protection around themselves and cleanse themselves and their homes of negative energy. Again, the power is created by your intention and belief, not just the tool.

How to make your own wand

A wand can be made of anything you like, but most witches will use natural materials such as wood, crystal or metal. If using metal, gold is good for love, silver helps to develop psychic abilities, steel helps with healing and protection, tin is good for luck and copper is ideal for attracting abundance.

A beginner witch is usually advised to create their own wand from a branch of a tree, such as an oak, birch, beech or pine tree. You will often find fallen branches near a tree, but if you can't, before you cut a branch, ask permission from the tree, and make sure you say thank you. Your branch should be around 30cm (12 inches) in length. Anything bigger than this and you will have trouble holding it. It doesn't have to be straight; in fact, some of the best wands are a little wonky.

If using a branch for your wand, you might need to allow it to dry out. Tree branches can hold a lot of moisture, so leave it in a warm room for a few days. Once dry, strip back the bark and then sand down the stick so that it's nice and smooth. Make sure you sand down any spikes or knobbly parts to protect your fingers when you use it. Some people like to apply a layer of clear gloss varnish to their wand once it's been sanded down.

Now you have your branch, you can gather whatever materials you wish to decorate it with. These should be as natural as possible, such as feathers, stones, twine, crystals or stones carved with rune symbols. You could also use personal items belonging to you, such as earrings or rings.

Have fun decorating your wand however you like! There are lots of ideas on Pinterest and Etsy. Of course, you can always purchase a wand if you want to, but I think it's more personal and fun to create your own. If you are thinking about buying a ready-made wand, choose one that you are automatically drawn to, and remember that once you bring it into your home, you must cleanse it of any past energy by submerging it in a glass of salt water and allowing it to dry before using it.

Once you are happy with your finished wand, it's a good idea to sleep with it under your pillow, so that it forms a connection to you while you're sleeping. You should soon feel a connective energy between you and your wand.

As with any of your tools, it's always advisable not to lend them to others because they can absorb another person's energy.

Tarot cards

Most witches don't tend to use Tarot cards in their spells, or if they do, they will just use one to help them focus or meditate on the spell they wish to perform. Tarot cards, runes, oracle cards, etc. are all just additional divination tools that witches may use, but you don't need them to cast spells.

As you progress on your path of witchery, you will soon notice that your intuition becomes more powerful as you tap in to the universe. This is the ideal time to invest in a deck of Tarot cards, runes or oracle cards, as they will help you to answer questions you might have or give you guidance and advice about a particular situation – but as I said, they are not an essential tool.

THE STAR

JUSTICE

THE LOVERS

A CAULDRON

Traditionally, a witch's cauldron was a tool used to mix up the ingredients for spells. It was also used for burning rituals and as somewhere for witches to hold offerings to their ancestors or goddesses. Most witches today will own a cauldron of some sort because they are just so handy for performing spells, particularly if they require fire.

Cauldrons would originally have been made from clay and later cast iron, and would have just been seen as another cooking pot to hang over the fire. Today you can buy iron cauldrons, but they can get quite expensive, and I think it's quite good fun to make your own.

HOW TO MAKE YOUR OWN CAULDRON

If you want to have a go at making your own cauldron, you will need:

- a large fireproof bowl or pot
- black heat-resistant paint
- a paintbrush
- fireproof decorative symbols (optional)
- a pinch of salt

You can often find large old cooking pots in thrift stores. Anything that is made out of iron, clay or ceramic is fine, so long as it is fire/heatproof. If you're creative, you could have a go at making your own cauldron out of clay and then ask a potter to dry it properly for you.

Clean the pot and leave it outside overnight to get rid of any negative energy that might be left inside it from the previous owner. Next, paint a coat of black paint evenly all over the outside and inside of the pot and leave to dry. Do this three times so that it has a good layer of protection.

If you wish to decorate your cauldron, make sure the decorations and glue you use are fire/heatproof. Alternatively, you could use a silver/gold permanent marker to decorate your cauldron with runes or a pentagram sign.

When you're happy with your cauldron, sprinkle a pinch of salt inside it to bless it. Now it is ready to use.

WITCHY GARDENS

Wicca is all about nature, and one of the main elements a witch relies on is herbs. While herbs are readily available from supermarkets these days, growing your own herb garden is ideal because the herbs will be fresh and ready to use at any time.

When your herbs are ready to harvest, be sure to pick a few and dry them on a sunny windowsill. You can then chop them and place them in herb containers, so that you always have herbs on hand when a spell requires it.

You don't have to be particularly green-fingered to create a herb garden. You can grow a large range of herbs indoors on your kitchen windowsill. If you don't want to grow herbs from seed, you can simply buy small planted pots of nursery herbs from garden centres or supermarkets and then repot them into larger plant containers so that they can grow and flourish. Do this, and you will have a never-ending supply of herbs ready for your spells.

Below is a list of the most common herbs a witch will need.

BASIL

Basil is closely related to the mint family. It has a lovely aroma and is often used to ward off viruses and infections. In witchcraft, basil is excellent for protection spells, love spells, money spells and prosperity. This plant is a good all-rounder to use if you don't have a particular specified herb to hand. Basil likes to grow either in a container or planted directly into the ground, but it does like the sunshine, so make sure you put it in a sunny spot. If you're planting basil outside, it prefers to be near vegetables rather than other herbs.

BAY

If you want a ready supply of fresh bay leaves, you can grow your own bay tree. Bay leaves are used in a number of spells including wish spells and protection spells, and can be used to enhance psychic abilities.

Bay trees are best planted in the spring and can be grown in a container or directly in the ground. However, they do take a while to get started, so I would advise you buy some bay leaves while your bay tree is getting established.

CHAMOMILE

Chamomile is known as a relaxant, and we see it used in a lot of teas to promote sleep and relaxation. In the world of Wicca, chamomile is ideal for spells to do with banishing anxiety and depression, as well as for spells for attracting peace and happiness into your life and releasing negative energy. Many witches will dry chamomile and use it in herb bundles for smoke cleansing and banishing rituals.

Chamomile is like mint – it loves to grow, so make sure you have a big container, or if you're planting it in your garden, ensure it has enough space to flourish. This herb is very thirsty during the summer and likes to have some shade.

CHIVES

Chives are associated with male energy and are a good for banishing spells, breaking hexes or for protecting yourself. Chives have also been found to have healing properties and can help fight off viral infections. Many insects don't like the smell of chives, so they can be a good pest-repellent too.

As chives don't spread out when they grow, they're ideal if you have limited space. This herb grows quickly; the more you harvest it, the faster it will grow. Wait until the chives are around 15cm (6 inches) tall, then you can cut and dry them to use in your spells.

DILL

Dill is thought to aid digestion and is often used to add flavour to soups and salads. It's also one of those plants that helps to reduce blood pressure and boost your immune system. Dill is used for love spells, warding off bad energy, healing, banishing spells, protection spells and ensuring karma is served.

If looked after, dill will grow all year round and can either be planted in a pot or directly in the earth. It likes sunshine, so make sure it gets plenty and you should get many harvests per year from this plant.

LAVENDER

Lavender is used in the beauty industry in oils, creams and perfumes, and it is also known as a relaxing and soothing plant. In spellcasting, it is ideal for cleansing, love spells, banishing anxiety and enhancing clairvoyance. Like basil, lavender is one of those herbs that is a good all-rounder to have on hand.

Lavender is a sun-worshipper and likes dry soil. It does, however, need good drainage. During the winter, lavender stems become 'woody'. This is the time to cut it right back so that you get a good harvest the following summer.

mint

There are several varieties of mint, but the most popular ones for a witch to grow are spearmint, peppermint and lemon mint. According to folklore, mint gets its name from the Greek nymph Minthe, who was the mistress of Hades. When his wife Persephone discovered their affair, either Persephone or her mother Demeter turned Minthe into the plant we know as mint.

Mint is very popular in the world of Wicca. Not only does it have lots of natural healing properties, but it is also used in a lot of prosperity spells (and it's a good fly deterrent, too!). A word of warning, though: mint grows very fast, and if you plant it directly in the ground, it will spread all over your garden. The best way to grow this plant is in a large pot, either indoors or outdoors.

MUGWORT

Mugwort has been used to boost energy, and in witchcraft it is perfect for protection spells. Witches who travel often place a sprig of mugwort in their shoes to protect them from harm and ensure a safe journey. This herb is also good to use in spells that require a specific moon phase, and it helps us to tap in to our psychic abilities too. In folklore, mugwort is associated with the goddess Diana, so is perfect for female witches.

Whether you plant mugwort in a container or straight into the ground, it will be quite happy, but it does like plenty of sunshine and the soil should have good drainage.

NETTLES

While you have to be careful with nettles due to their stinging potential, this is an ideal plant to grow to protect your home and keep negative people at bay. Nettles have been used in wines and cordials for years, but in witchcraft they are used to ward off anything evil that may try to come near you.

I would advise growing nettles in a pot because they spread like wildfire. If you have a nettle bush in your garden, just trim it back when it gets a bit out of hand. Make sure you wear gloves when harvesting or handling nettles because they do sting!

OREGANO

Oregano is one of those herbs that you tend to see in everyone's kitchen because it adds flavour to pretty much everything. In witchcraft, it is used in protection spells and has been shown to boost happiness and creativity. As it is associated with the planet Venus, oregano is particularly beneficial for female witches to use in their spells.

This plant requires planting in direct sunlight and well-drained soil, but it can happily grow on a sunny windowsill. It's also known as a natural insect repellent.

PARSLEY

Parsley is commonly used in soups and fish dishes, but it is also perfect to use in healing and love spells. It's a good herb to harvest, chop and dry, but because of its long stems, it is also ideal for use in smoke cleansing or tying into your broomstick to aid healing within the home.

This is another herb that is happy in a plant pot on your kitchen windowsill. A word of warning: while it does like the sunshine, it doesn't like to get too hot and will wilt quickly if it's in direct sunlight.

ROSEMARY

Rosemary is a versatile herb with a potent aroma, which is why it is used often in the beauty industry. This herb is another all-rounder, and one that every witch will use when casting spells. It has many properties, including cleansing, attracting happiness, promoting honesty and improving memory for exams. It's often used for smoke cleansing.

Rosemary likes to be planted near sage or vegetables, but you can also plant it in a pot in the kitchen. It thrives in the sunshine but does well in most climates.

SAGE

Sage has a distinctive smell and is often used for smoke cleansing, combined with rosemary, lavender and the like. As well as being a natural cleansing herb, sage promotes wisdom, knowledge and healing, and has the power to bring out our psychic abilities. Sage likes to be near rosemary but not many other herbs, so it's best to grow it in a pot rather than directly in the earth. Sage is also a perennial plant, so it will keep growing year after year.

When harvesting sage for smoke cleansing (see page 36), it's best to cut the plant when it's about 15cm (6 inches) in length. Dry it in the sunlight or a warm area, such as an airing cupboard – this will preserve the aroma. If you don't like smoke cleansing, you can grind dry sage and add it to water to make a nice cleansing spray, or add it to your bath to help you find the wisdom to solve any problems you may be experiencing.

THYME

Folklore states that thyme is the herb of good blessings. It is used in spells for courage, strength and protection from evil, so it's an excellent herb to use in karma magic.

Thyme is a relatively quick-growing plant that is happy in the ground or in a pot. It's really easy to grow as long as you give it plenty of sunshine and heat.

OTHER WITCHY KITCHEN ESSENTIALS:

Here are some additional ingredients to consider adding to your witchy pantry:

Cinnamon
Cinnamon is mainly grown in Sri Lanka. It is quite challenging to grow due to the climate and soil it requires, which is why I suggest you buy a jar of it from a supermarket. Cinnamon is used in protection and happiness spells. Some witches blow cinnamon through the front door (from the outside in) on the first of the month to promote a good month ahead.

Holly
This evergreen spiky-leafed plant is excellent to use in protection and banishing spells. Holly can be grown in the garden or in pots, and is also found in woodlands, fields, etc. It's worth keeping a few holly leaves in a jar for when you need an extra boost of karma magic. Although the holly bush is evergreen, the leaves brown quickly once harvested, so holly isn't very good for drying and preserving.

Pepper
Black pepper is a must for banishing spells and protecting yourself and your family from harm.

Salt
Salt is one of the main ingredients you will need as a witch. It is used mainly for protection, and you will often find a witch casting a salt circle whenever she performs a spell or a ritual. It doesn't matter if your salt comes from Himalaya or a supermarket, it will have the same effect on your spells.

Make a herb bundle

Smoke cleansing by burning herb bundles is a way to cleanse the energy around you, and although you can buy these bundles, they are so easy to make. Traditionally, the main herb for these bundles is sage and then you can add whatever herbs/plants you prefer.

Gather a handful of fresh sage and any other herbs that you like the smell of. You can include flowers, lavender, cinnamon sticks or vanilla pods – whatever you fancy. You should cut your herbs so that they are all around 15cm (6 inches) in length.

You must dry your herbs completely before burning. Do this by hanging your harvested herbs in a warm room for a couple of days. You will know when they are completely dried out because they will look like dead plants.

Once your herbs are dry, gather them up together into a bunch and secure them with some natural string or garden twine. Don't use synthetic string because it will give off toxic fumes. You will need to wrap the twine or string tightly around the whole bundle to ensure it doesn't fall apart.

When you have your bunch of herbs all secured together, leave it to dry for another two days to make extra sure that there is no moisture left in the bundle.

To cleanse an area, simply light one end of your dried herb bundle with a match, lighter or candle. Allow the flame to burn for a moment before blowing it out. Your bundle should now produce a fragrant smoke. Walk around the room, letting the smoke drift around. Pay extra attention to the corners of rooms, as this is where stagnant energy accumulates. You can cleanse any space – your car, your home or your office.

Once you have finished, turn the bundle upside down on a non-flammable plate to extinguish any heat. Once it's cooled down, you can put it away to use again when you need it.

GODDESS POWER

Most faiths or religions worship a god,
goddess or other spiritual figure. In
Hinduism, for example, believers worship
their favourite gods, goddesses and deities,
who each have their own stories, handed
down from generation to generation, while
Christians believe in Jesus, the son of God,
and will worship and pray to him.

In Wicca, people tend to be much more
open with regards to who they worship. To
worship a deity in this context simply means
to call upon them for help with a spell.

There are many goddesses, far too many to
mention in this book, whom you can call
upon to help you when you are practising
karma magic, but the ones I have listed below
are some of the most popular and powerful
to honour when spellcasting.

The Triple Goddess

The Triple Goddess is made up of three different female deities representing the divine feminine power in women. They are usually illustrated as a waxing, full and waning moon because they are associated with the moon's changing phases, and they also represent a woman's changing phases throughout her lifetime – the Maiden, the Mother and the Crone. You can call upon any one of these goddesses individually or upon all three, depending on your requests. Witches traditionally celebrate and give thanks to the Triple Goddess on 6 January.

The Maiden

The Maiden represents the young woman who is just starting out on her life journey. She is associated with new beginnings. Witches will call upon her to help with spells such as success for a new business, a new relationship or a new chapter in their life. The Maiden can be called upon at any time of the year, but especially during the spring months.

The Mother

The Mother represents the adult and fertile/maternal woman. She is called upon to help with protection and fertility spells. The Mother is all loving and comforting, just as an earth mother should be. The Mother can be called upon at any time of the year, but is especially powerful during the summer.

The Crone

The Crone represents wisdom and is at the height of womanhood. She is wise and is called upon to help offer guidance and intuition. Often when she called upon, witches will suddenly get ideas that they haven't thought about before. The Crone is also blessed with psychic abilities and will be able to help a witch enhance her skills in this area. The Crone can be called upon at any time of the year, but is especially powerful in autumn and winter.

The Horned God

Just as the Triple Goddess is associated with the power of the feminine, the Horned God deals with the masculine side of things. He represents fairness, harmony and protection, and is more of a father figure. Many witches will call upon the Horned God to help them if they feel they have been cursed or hexed, or to ask him to assist if a spell requires a more forceful power. The Horned God is connected to the Samhain (Halloween) sabbat, so sabbat, so this is the ideal time to call on him.

OTHER GODDESSES

BRIDGID

Bridgid is a Celtic goddess and the daughter of Dagda, the god of life and death. She appears in Irish mythology and is also known as Mary of the Gael or Brig. Bridgid is associated with two sisters, also called Bridgid, so it's been suggested that she is in fact a triple deity. Her festival day is 1 February, which is the Pagan festival of Imbolc, a time for celebrating that spring is on the way.

Bridgid was known as both a fire and water goddess. She is a fighter and protector, and is said to be worshipped by musicians, poets and writers the world over. She is also a healer, so she is the ideal goddess to call upon if you are dealing with a broken heart. Because she is a fierce protector, she will help to keep you safe when you ask her for assistance.

FREYA (FREYJA)

Freya is one of the most recognized goddesses. She originates from Norse mythology and is illustrated as a beautiful woman with long blond hair. She is also known to be a shapeshifter, and legend states that she travelled around in a carriage pulled by cats.

In witchcraft, you should call on the help of Freya when casting spells to do with love, fertility, beauty, sex and war. She's like having your biggest supporter on speed dial, and will help to fight your battles while remaining graceful and calm. Freya is a sun-worshipper, so call upon her during the Litha sabbat (summer solstice) to give more power to your spells.

FRIGG

Frigg is a Norse goddess. Legend has it that Frigg gave birth to her son Balder, whom she was very protective of – to the point of travelling the world to inform everyone not to harm her son. However, Balder ended up being killed by his own brother. Frigg was said to have visited the Underworld to strike a deal to release her son's soul back to her.

In Wicca, Frigg symbolizes family, protection and nurturing. She is called upon to help with spells that include protecting yourself or those you love. If you call upon Frigg during the Ostara sabbat (20 March), she will be very powerful to you.

ISIS

Isis is an ancient Egyptian goddess that most people will have heard of. She is the goddess of pretty much everything! She is worshipped as a mother figure and a powerful sorceress and healer. Isis does not tolerate threats, so she is the perfect deity to call upon if you feel threatened in anyway. She is pretty ruthless and will protect you forevermore if you call upon her for help. She also does not suffer fools easily, and will help you to see through the veil of anyone trying to deceive you. Witches celebrate on the Yule sabbat (21 December), otherwise known as the winter solstice.

LAKSHMI

Lakshmi, also known as Shri, is one of the great goddesses celebrated in Hinduism and is often called upon by witches to help with wealth, fortune and prosperity. She is depicted as having four arms and hands, holding a lotus flower in one, and she often has elephants or tigers by her side. You can call on Lakshmi for anything to do with wealth, good fortune and shopping. In India she is typically celebrated in October and November, during the Diwali festival of lights.

LUNA

Luna is the ancient Roman goddess of the moon and is the sister of Sol, the sun god. As the moon goddess, Luna is believed to be one of the most powerful goddesses to call upon. Because she controls our ocean tides, fishermen and sailors will call upon her for protection while they are at sea. She is depicted as a woman in a flowing dress, often riding a horsedrawn chariot. Because she oversees the moon's phases, she is often drawn with a crescent moon on her forehead, in her hair or on her dress. Luna is part of a triple deity and represents the Mother of the trio, along with Proserpina, the Queen of the Underworld, who represents the Maiden and Hecate, who represents the Crone. You can call upon Luna to protect you from harm, to make you more creative and to keep you safe when travelling. Her celebration day is 31 March, when it is believed that her powers are at their peak

MORRÍGAN

Morrígan is a powerful goddess of Irish origin. She is associated with war, battles, fate and death. Morrígan is also a shapeshifter and is likely to change into a black crow. In Irish folklore, Morrígan is said to have two sisters, Badb and Macha, whom she will call upon to help her fight her battles. Her symbols are often seen on books, statues and jewellery in the form of traditional Celtic symbols such as the Celtic knot and the Tree of Life. Morrígan's celebration day is 1 November, which is part of the Samhain sabbat. As a warrior, she is an ideal goddess to call upon to help deliver karma to anyone who has done you wrong.

BEL

Bel (or Belenus, to use his full name) is the god of light, and lends his name to Beltane, the Wiccan May festival that falls between the spring equinox and the summer solstice. It is believed that Bel has Celtic origins. Although he is associated with fire and light, he was not a sun god, but more of an earthly protector of cattle. According to folklore, Belenus created two fires on either side of his cattle to protect them from being harmed. Beltane is celebrated on 1 May because it signals the movement from darkness to light, and the beginning of summer.

MOON PHASES

The moon plays an important role in the life of a witch. Witches will use the power and energy of the moon to help us with our spellcasting. A waning moon is particularly helpful when you're performing karma spells. Each moon phase has its own energy, and while it's not always necessary to cast a spell on a particular moon phase, doing so can enhance certain spells, making them more powerful and hastening the results. But remember: the most important part of magic is your intent.

The moon's gravitational pull affects the tides of our oceans, and it is also known to be beneficial to plants and nature – studies have shown that plants can flourish when planted during certain moon phases, particularly the new and full moon. It's also been well documented that different phases of the moon can influence us as humans. The old-fashioned word 'lunatic' comes from the Latin word *lunaticus* meaning 'of the moon', referring to madness, and it's been known that people's behaviour, mental state and emotional wellbeing can be impacted during the time of a full moon. Many law-enforcement departments will tell you that they notice a significant rise in crimes during a full-moon period. So, you can see just how powerful our beautiful moon can be.

The moon goes through eight phases every 29.5 days, which is the time it takes for the moon to orbit the Earth. These phases are the new moon, the waxing crescent, the first quarter, the waxing gibbous, the full moon, the waning gibbous, the third quarter and finally the waning crescent.

However, most spellcasters will only refer to the four main phases of the moon: the new moon, the waxing crescent, the full moon and the waning crescent. Each of these moon phases lasts between three and ten days. This means that if you forget to cast a full-moon spell on a full-moon day, you will still have about a week after the full moon to perform the spell before the phase changes again.

Below are the four main phases of the moon for you to refer to when doing karma magic.

The new moon

The new moon is the first of the monthly moon phases. Ironically, despite being called the new moon, it isn't actually visible in the sky because we can only see the moon thanks to the illumination of the sun, and in this phase the side of the moon facing Earth is not lightened by the sun – but fear not, it is still there!

The new moon is a time for new beginnings, and is the perfect time for performing karma spells when you just want a fresh start and to forget about the past. New-moon spells are good for long-term spells that require a bit of time to work, because as the month progresses, so too does the momentum for the power of your spell. Use this phase of the moon for manifesting the best possible outcome for yourself, and to seek out new opportunities and inspiration if you feel stuck in life.

The waxing moon

The waxing moon is when the moon looks as though it is increasing in size. In this phase, the moon looks like a D-shaped crescent in the sky. It is during this time that witches will cast manifestation spells. It is the ideal time to cast spells for anything that you wish to grow, whether you are seeking prosperity and luck, or casting a spell for more confidence so that you can stand up for yourself or when you have an exam or a test coming up. It's also a good time to ask for help with making decisions that you are unsure about. This time of the month is dedicated to positive changes and growth.

The full moon

Magic performed during the full moon is the most powerful of all magic, which is why you often see it depicted in movies and books as the time that witches will gather to perform spells. It is the time of the month when the moon's gravitational pull is at its most powerful. Because the moon affects our emotions, it is also a time when people can be unpredictable.

Any spell performed during a full moon will be more powerful than at any other time of the month, and it's a time when anything goes, so it's ideal for any spells you wish to cast. Karmic spells are particularly powerful during the full-moon phase.

If you leave a jar of water out overnight during a full moon, the water will be energized by the moon's power. This is known as 'moon water' and is very useful to use in spells that require water. It's also the best time to take a bath (known as 'full-moon bathing') because it will release any negative energy that may have attached itself to you.

The waning moon

The waning moon comes after the full moon. This is when the illumination decreases and the moon begins her new cycle. Waning moons have always been associated with banishment and getting rid of something that is interfering in your life. This moon phase is ideal for karma spells, and you will notice that many of the banishment spells in this book will suggest you cast them during this time.

The waning-moon phase is also a great time for cleaning and cleansing yourself and your home, so if you'd like to do some smoke cleansing (see page 36), this is the time to get out a herb bundle and clear away any negative energy you feel. If you need to release something, someone or a bad habit from your life, cast your spell during the waning-moon phase, and let the energy of the moon help you to get rid of things that no longer serve you.

Blue Moon

Once every couple of years, we get to see a second full moon in one month. This is known as a Blue Moon, and it's where the phrase 'once in a Blue Moon' comes from, which refers to something being quite rare. When you have a month with a second full moon in it, your spells will be at their most powerful.

PART TWO:
THE SPELLS

ABOUT KARMA SPELLS

Now that we've covered the basics of witchcraft and karma, we are going to look at spells that are specifically designed for karma. As previously mentioned, karma is not what we have been led to believe – no one has the power to make someone die suddenly or have a nasty accident. The laws of karma are much more complicated.

The spells in this book are designed to protect you from those who wish you harm. This can even include yourself; sometimes your own mind is your worst enemy and will convince you that you are not good enough, leading to you feeling uncomfortable in your own skin. Or sometimes it is society that convinces you that you are strange or unworthy. Ultimately, however, all the spells in this book are about you and looking after your wellbeing, rather than destroying someone who has hurt you.

Remember: those people who set out to hurt you will have their own karma to deal with, so don't be tempted to dabble in black magic to get your own back; the universe will take care of that for you.

The second thing I'd like to mention is that although many of the spells in this book will have ingredients listed to use, if you can't find the correct ingredient, do not worry.

As explored earlier, true magic is all about intention (see page 16), and it's quite alright if you have to substitute one ingredient for another. For example, if a spell requires black pepper and you don't have any to hand, think what other ingredients you might be able to use, such as charcoal from your barbecue or nettles from a field outside. Always go with your intuition, because it is never wrong.

SPELL PREPARATION

Now, let's get to the fun part! When spellcasting, it's always a good idea to begin by protecting yourself. You can do this by sitting quietly for a few minutes before beginning a spell and imagining a white light coming down from the sky, hitting your head and washing over your entire body like a fountain. Visualize this light wrapping around you and sealing you in for a few minutes. This is your protection blanket, and it means that zero negative energy can enter and disturb you.

A few basic safety notes: always take care when working with naked flames, and make sure you place any candles in a suitable holder. Use gloves when handling nettles, avoid ingredients to which you are allergic, and always dispose of materials in the appropriate way.

Look through the different spells for one that you feel suits your situation or will help you. Technically, there are no limits to the number of spells that you can cast, but it's best to try to stick to one spell per day. This is because if you cast too many, your energy may feel depleted afterwards, or you may find your spells are not as powerful as the energy has become a little confused.

Finally, if a spell requires a particular day or moon phase, try to stick to it as best you can to give it optimum power.

CREATING YOUR OWN SPELLS

As I mentioned earlier in the book, it is not necessary to have lots of witchy paraphernalia. This is always a particular bugbear of mine, because Wicca and witchcraft should be about nature, freedom, intention and intuition, not rules and regulations. Many will disagree and tell you that you're using the wrong ingredient or casting during the wrong moon phase, but I feel that when you start imposing rules, you lose your natural magical abilities, and it becomes nothing more than another dictated religion.

While all the spells in this book have been proven to work and are great fun to cast, one of the quickest ways to banish something or someone from your life is to literally write the problem on a piece of paper and burn it. Don't think that you have to spend a fortune on products to be able to cast spells.

If you wish to create your own spells or adapt one of the spells in this book, it will still work – in fact, it will be more powerful because it is coming from you personally. The spells in this book are all tried and tested and are what have worked for me and many others, but if you don't have a particular ingredient or herb, or you forget to mention a particular goddess when casting your spell, please do not worry. If a spell states that you need dried mint and you don't have any, use a piece of mint chewing gum, or a mint-flavoured sweet. Just go with what you have available at the time. The most powerful

spells are ones that you create yourself, and the more passionate you are and the more personal you can make a spell, the more effective it will be.

The only one rule I would stipulate when learning about spellcasting and witchcraft is that you try to keep it to yourself. As we know, everything and everyone is made up of energy, and if that energy doesn't match our own, it can have a negative effect on us. Some people are against witchcraft because they know little to nothing about it. By trying to educate them, you will find that their energy will affect yours and make you question your own powers. Plus, there's something quite thrilling about secretly knowing that you have this magical power within you!

Magic is also supposed to be fun, so make it so. When someone does you wrong in life, feel happy that you now have the tools and training to make them go away, while at the same time feeling assured that you are protecting yourself.

Hopefully this book will teach you to learn how, with a little magic, you can make sure that those who have crossed you will have their karma delivered to them – but, more importantly, I hope you learn that you are the one in control of your own destiny, and you have the power to manifest a peaceful and protected life.

Freeze Spell

PURPOSE

To freeze someone toxic out of your life

WHEN TO CAST

Any day and time during a waning-moon phase

YOU WILL NEED

a black candle

a piece of paper (postcard size)

a black marker pen

an ice-cube tray with at least 13 moulds

a freezer

a bowl or cauldron

Darren will no longer
contact me again

Truth be told, life will always throw someone or something that you don't particularly want into your path, and sometimes no amount of hinting or showing them the door helps. It's like they're oblivious and simply can't take the hint. Often this can be just a very annoying neighbour, or it could be something more serious such as an ex who just won't leave you alone. This is where the freeze spell comes into play – by helping you 'freeze' a problem.

WHAT TO DO

It's best to perform this ritual during a waning-moon phase, but if you can't wait, then any day of the month will be fine. The main thing that gives any spell power is your intention.

First of all, light your black candle and set the intention that you are protected and that you are performing this spell for the good of all and in particular for your own peace of mind.

Think of a sentence that sums up your intention for the spell. For example, if your intention is to stop your ex from contacting you again, your sentence might be: 'Darren will no longer contact me.'

Now take your piece of paper and black marker and write only the first letter of each word in the sentence. So, for the example above, you'd write: 'D W N L C M.'

You can make your sentence as long or as short as you wish. The reason you only write the first letter of each word is because witches would often write in code so that no one else could tell what their spells were referencing.

Once you are happy with your freeze sentence, write the letters 'S M I B' underneath it. This stands for 'So mote it be,'

which is a way of saying your spell is ready to go, and you have faith that it will work.

Fill 13 of the moulds in your ice-cube tray with tap water and rip the paper into 13 equal pieces. This shows that you are done with this problem and are sending it out to the universe to deal with now. Place one piece of paper into each filled ice-cube mould, and continue until you've used all 13 pieces.

Blow out the candle and say, 'The spell is cast.' You can keep this candle for future freeze spells.

Transfer the ice-cube tray to your freezer and leave it for 48 hours.

Once the ice cubes are fully frozen, take the tray out of the freezer and pop out each of the 13 ice cubes into a bowl or cauldron.

In your garden (or in a plant pot, if you don't have a garden), scatter the ice cubes in with the plants. The ice will melt, and the paper will eventually decompose, meaning the spell has worked and you should be free from whoever or whatever is bothering you.

If after 28 days the problem persists, repeat the spell once a day for the next seven days.

Graveyard Spell

PURPOSE

To return a curse to the hexer

WHEN TO CAST

Any day and time during a waning-moon phase

WHAT YOU NEED

3 tablespoons earth from either a graveyard or another town or country

a small dish

1 garlic clove, crushed

salt water

1 red chilli

a small mirror

a small black candle (a tealight will do)

salt

This is the spell to use if you feel as though everything that can go wrong is going wrong. Sometimes it's just one of those periods in life, but other times the reason can be traced back to someone else. It's a misconception that in order to curse another, you need to know about magic. Spells are all about intention and energy, and if someone feels hatred to you, this can often manifest as a curse, even though they haven't intentionally cast a spell on you.
This spell will return the curse or ill wishes to the person who sent it.

WHAT TO DO

Place all your items in front of you on a table and concentrate on your power to be able to return this curse back to the perpetrator.

Place the earth you've gathered into the small dish. Add the garlic and a few drops of salt water and mix into a muddy paste, then place the red chilli pepper on top of the mixture.

Now place the small mirror behind the dish so it is reflected in the mirror, and place the black candle in front of the dish. Take your salt and draw a salt circle around these items.

Dip the pinkie finger of your dominant hand into the muddy paste and draw a pentagram symbol (a five-sided star within a circle) on the small mirror. Now light your candle.

Stare into the mirror and say the following words:

To the person who wishes evil upon me, I return your harm to thee, times three.

All your intended evil can and will no longer harm me.

With the power of Isis, I return your curse to you with immediate effect.

So mote it be.

Stare into the flame of the candle and visualize the curse/intended harm being returned to the perpetrator. Allow the candle to burn down safely. After you've cast your spell, remove the chilli from the dish and scoop the earth from the dish into some toilet paper, then flush it down the toilet. Clean your mirror and blow away the salt circle. Dispose of the chilli somewhere away from your house. If there is any wax left over from the candle, put it in the bin. The spell is now complete, and any curse will be returned to its owner.

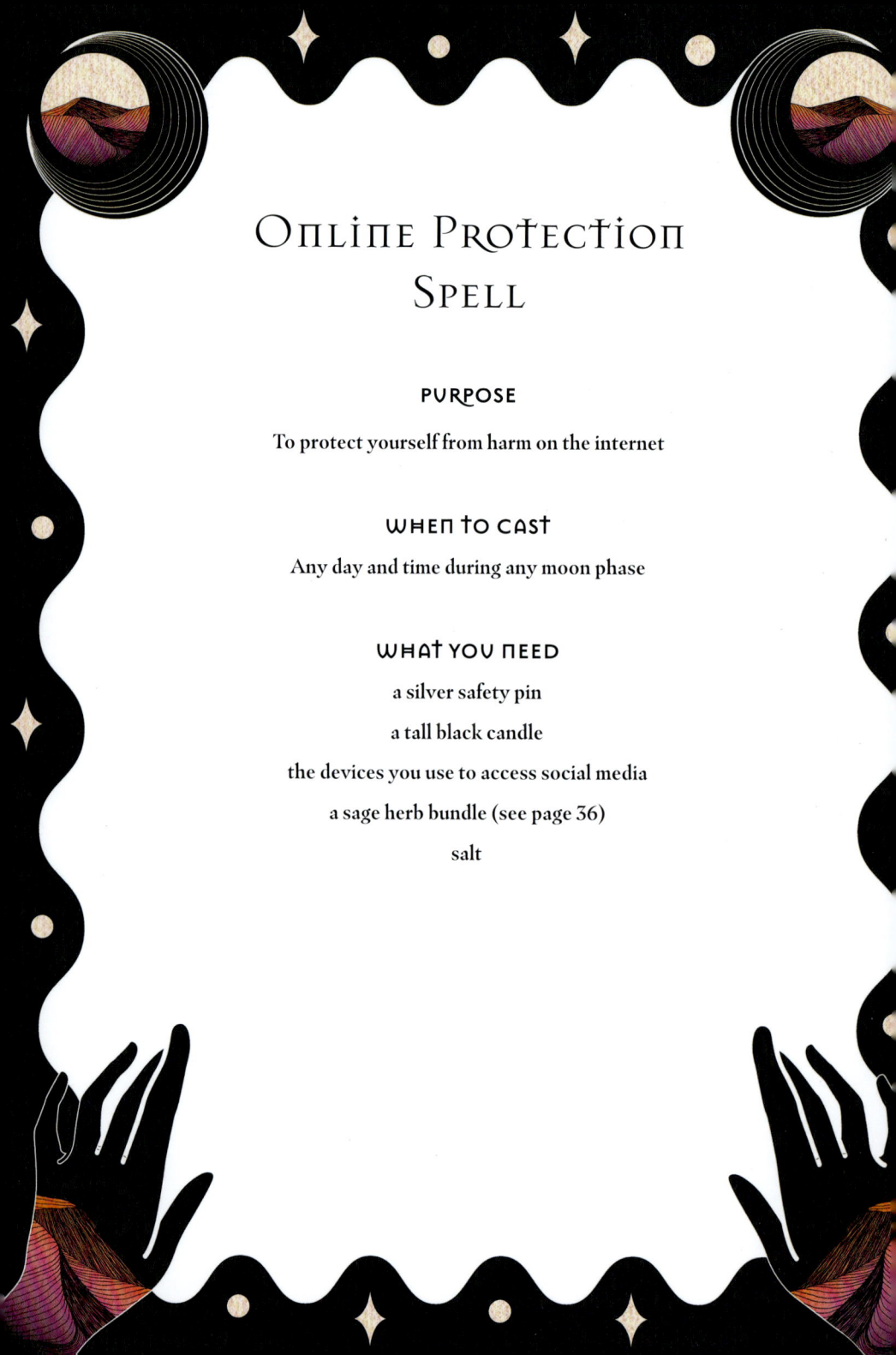

Online Protection Spell

PURPOSE

To protect yourself from harm on the internet

WHEN TO CAST

Any day and time during any moon phase

WHAT YOU NEED

a silver safety pin

a tall black candle

the devices you use to access social media

a sage herb bundle (see page 36)

salt

It's never nice when someone starts trolling you on social media. It's all well and good to be told to block and delete when someone is being nasty online, but it doesn't stop them from setting up multiple accounts to continue writing unpleasant things about you or sharing them with other people you know. And besides, why should you limit your online activity just because someone feels they can attack you? How dare they? If you're having problems with an online troll, or someone just won't leave you alone to enjoy your social media in peace, try this powerful spell to get rid of them once and for all.

WHAT TO DO

First, make sure you have blocked and deleted any troll contacts.

Take the silver safety pin and open it up. Use its point to engrave the side of the candle with the name or names of whoever has been trolling you (these can be their usernames).

Near the bottom of the candle, carve a pentagram symbol (a five-sided star within a circle), followed by the letters 'S M I B' ('So mote it be'). Stab the safety pin into the candle about halfway along its length.

Gather all your devices that you use for social media and place them in the middle of a desk or table – keep them switched on. Take the salt and draw two lines of salt across the table, one above your devices and the other below your devices. These are your boundary lines.

Place the candle next to your devices within the salt lines and light it. Light your herb bundle from the candle and waft the smoke around all your devices.

As you do so, say the following words out loud:

TODAY I SET MY ONLINE BOUNDARIES

NO LONGER WILL YOU BREAK THE LINE

ONLY LOVE AND GOOD CAN NOW ACCESS ME ONLINE.

THIS IS MY WORD, SO MOTE IT BE.

Stub out your herb bundle and then allow the candle to safely burn down completely. The safety pin should drop out when it has burned down halfway. Keep the pin to one side and, once the candle has burned down completely, close the pin. This means that the spell is now fixed. Keep the safety pin closed unless you need to repeat the spell in the future.

You can now clear away the salt, then turn off all your devices and restart them. You will now be protected from nasty online trolls. Repeat the spell as often as you need, but always remember to block and delete those who insist on bugging you.

Travel Safety Spell

PURPOSE

To protect yourself when travelling

WHEN TO CAST

Any day and time prior to travelling, during any moon phase

WHAT YOU NEED

a small blue crystal such as aquamarine, lapis lazuli or blue sapphire

a glass beaker

lavender oil

peppermint oil

a long sprig of lavender

a paper towel

Have you ever experienced a vacation from hell? The kind of trip where if something could go wrong, it did? Often when you're travelling to another place, your energy can get mixed up with that of every other traveller. Some of your fellow travellers might be projecting negative energy because their flight has been delayed or they've just had an argument with the check-in desk over their baggage allowance, and this energy is then absorbed by everyone around them. This can cause havoc if you're not protected.

WHAT TO DO

Whether it's a road trip in your car or you're going overseas, prior to travelling take the blue crystal of your choosing and wash it under the tap to clean and energize it in running water.

In the glass beaker, mix together 13 drops of lavender oil and 13 drops of peppermint oil. When the oils are thoroughly mixed, hold your crystal in the palm of your dominant hand until it begins to feel warm. Drop the crystal into the oil mixture, turning it to ensure the crystal is completely coated in the oils. Visualize this crystal being infused with the power to protect.

Place the crystal on the paper towel and pat it dry. Now take your sprig of lavender and wrap it around the crystal and tie it. If your crystal is too small for the lavender to wrap around it, you can just keep the lavender sprig in a small pouch with your crystal, but they should be kept together.

The spell is now complete. Every time you travel anywhere, you should take your protection crystal with you and invoke the goddess Luna, the protection goddess of travel, by visualizing her alongside you when you're travelling. Repeat this spell whenever you travel again.

Simple Binding
Spell

PURPOSE

To banish a specific person from your life

WHEN TO CAST

Any time on the first day of a waning-moon phase

WHAT YOU NEED

a small square of paper

a black marker pen

something small and personal relating to the person you want to bind, such as a strand of hair from their hairbrush or a sample of their handwriting (if you can't find anything suitable, then use a photo or a piece of paper with their name written on it)

some garden twine (not plastic)

A binding spell is a spell designed to help rid you of a person who is bothering you, or someone from whom you need to keep your distance for the good of your health. Contrary to popular belief, binding spells do not cause any harm to the other person, and they are not associated with dark or black magic. They are, however, a very effective way of preventing another person from contacting you or causing you trouble again.

WHAT TO DO

Take the small square of paper and draw a pentagram (see symbol below) with the black marker. Place the personal item of the person you wish to bind in the centre of the paper square and roll the paper into a tube. Take the twine and wrap it around the paper scroll several times, while visualizing the unwanted person being bound from getting near you again.

Tie the two ends of the garden twine with three knots so that the scroll is secure. Take the scroll to a body of flowing water such as a river, a canal or the sea. With your back to the river, say the following words:

[Name of the person], i now bind you from causing harm to me or anyone else.

You will no longer be able to enter my life.

This will be so.

Imagine that this person is tied up within the scroll. With your back to the water, throw the scroll over your right shoulder into the flowing water. Walk away and don't look back.

You will find that the person who has been bothering you will suddenly disappear from your life for good.

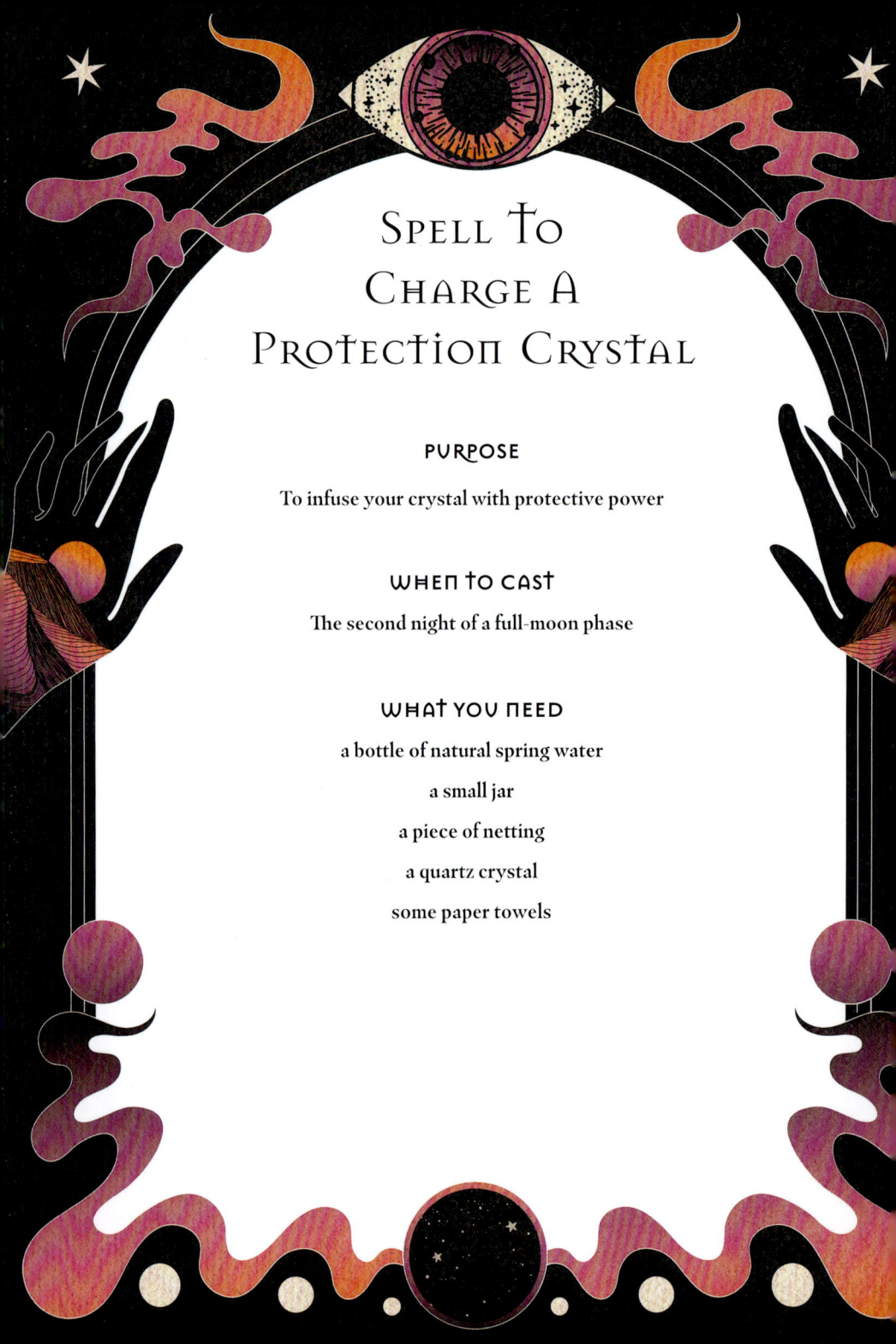

Spell To Charge A Protection Crystal

PURPOSE

To infuse your crystal with protective power

WHEN TO CAST

The second night of a full-moon phase

WHAT YOU NEED

a bottle of natural spring water

a small jar

a piece of netting

a quartz crystal

some paper towels

The best and most secret way to protect yourself from people with bad karma to spread is to carry a protection crystal with you when you are near them. Whether it's the office gossip, a family member or a frenemy who just won't leave you alone, a protection crystal will absorb any negative karmic energy being directed your way. For this protection spell, choose a crystal that you're particularly drawn to. The best protection crystals are black tourmaline, amethyst and clear quartz, but if you don't have one of these, just choose your favourite. This could be in a piece of jewellery or a stone on its own. Because this spell requires moon water and should be conducted on a full moon, you can gather up all your crystals and charge them all at the same time if you prefer.

WHAT TO DO

On the second night of the full-moon phase, when the moon is at her most powerful, take the lid off your spring water and pour it into your jar. Place the piece of netting across the top of the jar to stop any bugs getting into it.

Leave the jar (without a lid) somewhere safe in your garden overnight. If you don't have a garden, leave it on a windowsill from which the full moon is visible.

The following day, place your crystal in the jar of water and put the lid on it. Leave the crystal in the water until the full moon has gone (you can look up the date and length of the full moon on the internet).

Once the full moon has passed, take out your crystal and pat dry with the paper towels.

Your crystal is now charged by the power of the moon. Carry it with you every time you know you are going to encounter a hostile person. If that person is a work colleague, and you can place the crystal on your desk, so much the better. The crystal will now project protection and will repel people who add nothing of value to your life.

User-Loser Spell

PURPOSE

To banish someone who's been using you

WHEN TO CAST

Any day and time during a full-moon phase

WHAT YOU NEED

a small bunch of stinging nettles

a mug of hot water

a piece of paper and a pen

a Queen of Hearts playing card

3 silver sewing pins

It's horrible when it suddenly dawns on you that the person whom you thought was your ride-or-die turns out to be someone who has just used you, whether that's for money, sex, love, friendship, introductions that can help them in some way, or just to keep them amused until someone/something better comes along. This karma spell will ensure that the user becomes the loser. If you don't have nettles in your garden (see page 33), you can find them in a field or at the roadside, but take a pair of gloves with you as they do sting bare hands!

WHAT TO DO

Add the nettles to the mug of hot water. Leave to steep for 10 minutes.

While the nettles are brewing, write the initials of the person who has been using you on a piece pf paper. Place this piece of paper on top of the Queen of Hearts playing card and stab the three silver pins into the initials so that the pins go through both the paper and the card. Say the following words:

[Name], you will now feel my sting, i no longer allow you to use me for your own benefits.

This ends now and you will pay the price.

It is so.

Submerge the playing card, paper and pins in the mug of nettle water and leave it in there for 3 hours. If you have an item belonging to the person who has been using you, you can also sprinkle a few drops of the nettle water on to it.

After 3 hours strain the liquid from the cup down the sink and dispose of the contents in the bin. The person who has been using you will very soon disappear from your life and will eventually realize how badly they have behaved.

Narcissists' Nightmare Spell

PURPOSE

To protect you from a narcissist

WHEN TO CAST

Any day and time during a full-moon phase

WHAT YOU NEED

2 luggage labels with string

a black pen

a hole-punch

2 bay leaves

a witch's broom (see page 20)

You're very lucky if you've never encountered someone who is narcissistic enough to make you feel less than. It's very hard to regain your self-worth when someone has spent years putting you down, whether it's a parent, friend, work colleague, boss or partner. Just remember: that person will have carved out their own karma, so you don't need to put pins into an effigy of them. What you do need to do, however, is claim back your power and protect yourself so that you never become a victim of a narcissist again.

WHAT TO DO

Place one luggage label in front of you, and on it write the name of the person who has been abusing you. Below this, write any unkind words they have said to you. Punch a hole through the first bay leaf with your hole-punch, and add the leaf to your luggage label. Tie both the leaf and the label to your broomstick.

Sweep your floor with your broomstick, moving from one side of the hallway to the front door, and say the following:

**SWEEP, SWEEP, I SWEEP YOU AWAY,
YOUR WORDS WILL NEVER HURT ME AGAIN.**

**SWEEP, SWEEP, AWAY WITH YOUR STRIFE
NEVER AGAIN WILL YOU ENTER MY LIFE.**

Once you reach the threshold of your home, open the door and sweep the energy outside. Pull off the luggage label and bay leaf, and throw it in an outside bin. Bring your broom back indoors and close your front door. You should feel that the energy is much lighter now.

Sit back down and take the second luggage label. Write your name on it. Beneath your name, write the words: 'I am worthy.' Punch a hole into the second bay leaf with your

hole-punch and add this to the luggage label. Again, tie the label and the bay leaf to the stem of your broomstick.

Place your broom somewhere where you will see it every day, and leave it there for the next 28 days. You will feel a shift in energy and your self-worth will rocket after this.

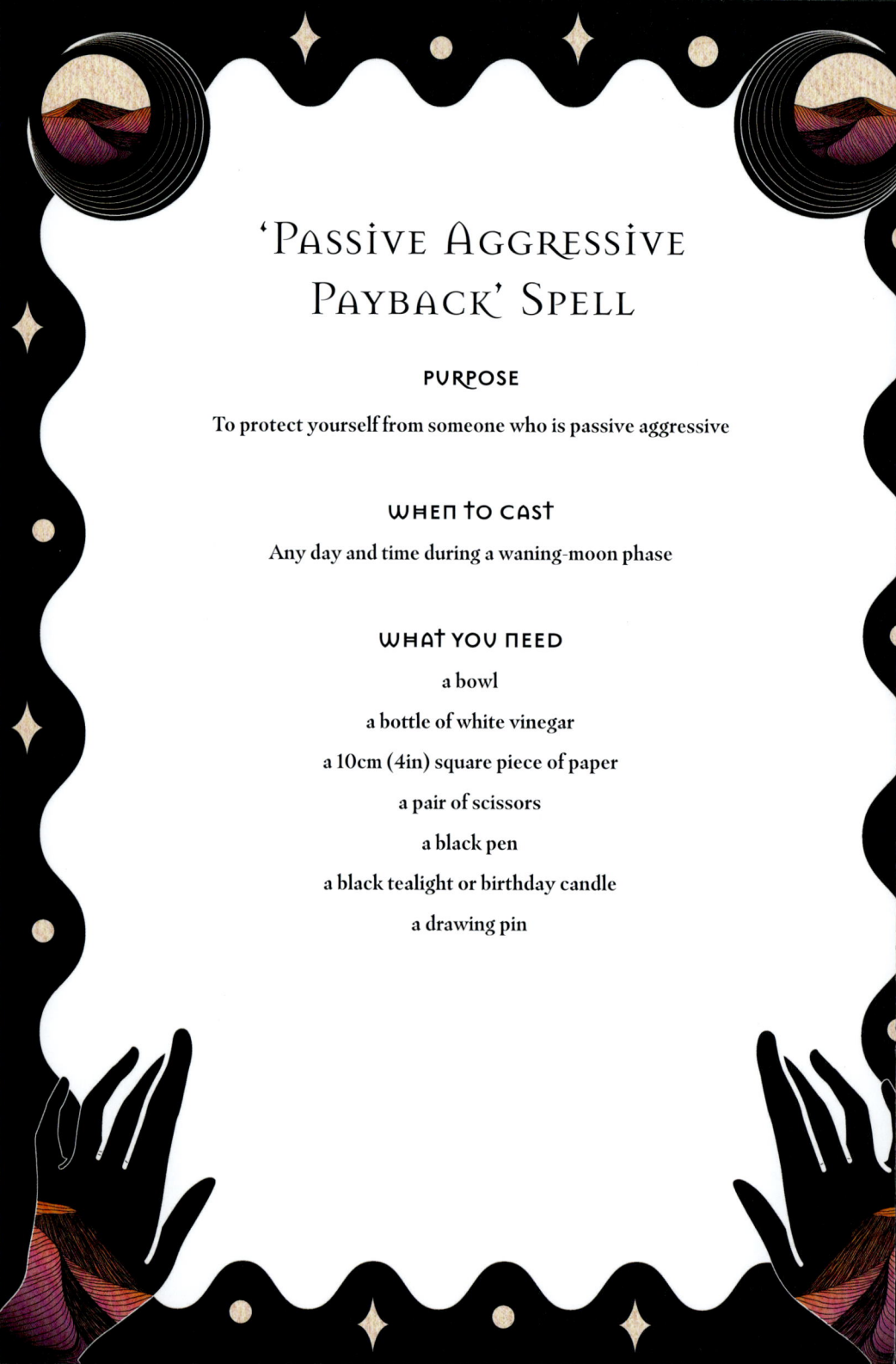

'Passive Aggressive Payback' Spell

PURPOSE

To protect yourself from someone who is passive aggressive

WHEN TO CAST

Any day and time during a waning-moon phase

WHAT YOU NEED

a bowl

a bottle of white vinegar

a 10cm (4in) square piece of paper

a pair of scissors

a black pen

a black tealight or birthday candle

a drawing pin

Some people cover up their nastiness by being passive aggressive. It is awful to be on the receiving end of snide comments or behaviour from someone who isn't mature enough to say what they're really thinking. This little spell will make them think twice before doing it again to you.

WHAT TO DO

To prepare this spell, fill the bowl with white vinegar, then add the paper to the bowl and let it soak for a few minutes until it's wet all over. Remove the paper from the bowl and place it somewhere warm to dry, such as a sunny windowsill.

Once your paper is dry, cut it into a triangle shape. In each corner of the triangle, draw a small circle with a dot in the middle of it. This represents the Egyptian power of the pyramid and the third eye.

With the black pen, write the full name of the person who is always passive aggressive towards you inside the triangle. Light your black candle and repeat the following words:

YOUR SARCASM AND AGGRESSION, DRESSED UP AS PLAY,
ARE NO LONGER WELCOME HERE TODAY.

BY THE POWER OF THE PYRAMID
AND THE POWER IN ME,
I BANISH YOUR AGGRESSION.

SO MOTE IT BE.

Allow the candle to safely burn down. Take the piece of paper and puncture a hole through the middle of their name with the pin, then pin it on a wall in a dark corner of your home.

The person's behaviour towards you will soon change for the better.

Report, Delete, Block Spell

PURPOSE

To get rid of an online stalker

WHEN TO CAST

Any day and time during any moon phase

WHAT YOU NEED

12 white tealight candles

12 bay leaves

a witch's broom (see page 20)

a large bag of pink Himalayan salt (available at most pharmacies)

Have you ever accepted a friend or follow request or swiped right without a second thought, only to end up with your very own online stalker? Anyone can be anyone when they're hiding behind a keyboard. If you've been a victim of someone who is not who they said they were, your first move must be to report, delete and then block them from contacting you. Next, you need to do a protection spell to keep yourself safe and to keep them away from you. This powerful little spell will ensure that they disappear from your life for good.

WHAT TO DO

Place 11 of your tealight candles in a large circle, then place the final candle in the middle of the circle. Visualize the feeling of the person who has been bothering you being gone from your life as you kiss each bay leaf and place it under a candle. Repeat this until all the candles have a bay leaf underneath them. Place your witch's broom at the top of the circle, a safe distance from the candles.

Light all the candles, working in an anticlockwise direction. As you do so, say the following words:

When all the candles have burned down, pick up the bay leaves and scatter them outside your home. Take the Himalayan salt and sprinkle it in every corner of your home, across the threshold and around your car, if you have one.

Take your broom and place it upside down by your front door. This will ensure that whoever has been bothering you will never come near your home, and the spell you have cast will make sure they no longer have any access to you.

BY ONE THE SPELL HAS BEGUN,
BY TWO I BRING TO YOU,
BY THREE I COMMAND THEE.
BY FOUR YOU LEAVE BY THE DOOR,
BY FIVE YOU NO LONGER THRIVE,
BY SIX I GRANT THIS WISH,
BY SEVEN MY SPELL IS CAST TO THE HEAVENS,
BY EIGHT I SIT AND WAIT,
BY NINE THE POWER IS MINE,
BY TEN WE BEGIN AGAIN,
BY ELEVEN I PROCLAIM,
BY TWELVE YOUR POWER HAS NO CONTROL OVER ME.

'Take Back My Power' Spell

PURPOSE

To reclaim your autonomy

WHEN TO CAST

Any day and time during any moon phase

WHAT YOU NEED

a silver sewing pin

a white tealight candle

a wand (see page 26) – or your finger will do

Sometimes other people can make us feel powerless. Whether it's a friend, a partner, a boss or a neighbour, there are some people in this world who seem to have the ability to intimidate and bully. Remember, hurt people hurt people, and they will get their karma served to them in some way. In the meantime, this little spell will help you to take back your power, making you feel less intimidated and more powerful around people who make you feel less than.

WHAT TO DO

This spell focusses on the Reiki power symbol Cho Ku Rei (pronounced 'Cho Koo Ray'), which is often used in healing therapy and means 'placing all the powers of the universe here' – so it's the ideal symbol to use to take back your power.

Find a quiet moment when you can be alone for a few minutes. Take your silver pin and use it to carefully engrave the Cho Ku Rei symbol (see below) into the top of the tealight candle.

Light the tealight and close your eyes while visualizing the heat from the flame of the candle giving you strength and power. Imagine you're turning into Superwoman. Take three deep breaths, then, with your wand or finger, draw the Cho Ku Rei symbol in the air 13 times, while chanting:

'CHO KU REI TO ME TODAY.'

When you've finished chanting, take one more deep breath and blow out the candle. You can reuse this candle whenever you feel you need to repeat the spell.

Anyone who now tries to overpower you will quickly discover that you are a force to be reckoned with.

'Return The Favour' Spell

PURPOSE

To send someone's bad energy back to them

WHEN TO CAST

Any day and time during a full-moon phase

WHAT YOU NEED

an airmail envelope (or a picture of one)

a red pen

a black pillar candle

a white pillar candle

ground black pepper

salt

a small hematite crystal

Most witches don't like the idea of revenge spells and would rather say they are 'returning the favour' to someone who has hurt or harmed them in some way. This spell will ensure that whoever has tried to bring destruction to your life will have that 'favour' returned to them.

WHAT TO DO

Gather your ingredients on a table where they can be undisturbed until the spell is complete. If you can't get hold of an airmail envelope, find an image of one and print it out. Use the red pen to write a letter to the person or people who have tried to destroy you, explaining that you are now returning the favour to them, and that they should never mess with a witch. Don't worry, you are not going to send this, so you can write whatever you feel like.

Once you've written your letter, place it in on the table with the two candles on either side. Draw a full circle of black pepper around the black candle. Around the white candle (which is for your protection), draw a full circle of salt. Place the hematite crystal on top of the airmail letter.

Light the white candle first, and say:

BY THE POWER OF THIS LIGHT, I CALL UPON THE UNIVERSE TO PROTECT ME FROM FURTHER DESTRUCTION FROM [NAME(s)].

Next, light the black candle and say:

BY THE POWER OF DARKNESS, I RETURN TO YOU ALL THE HARM YOU HAVE PROJECTED UPON ME, [NAME(s)].

FROM HERE ON, YOU WILL HAVE YOUR ENERGY DRAWN BACK TO YOU, AND RECEIVE WHAT YOU DESERVE.

AS I RETURN TO SENDER.

Allow both candles to safely burn down. Often you will find that the black candle will burn down faster. This is a sign that the bad energy is quickly being returned to the perpetrator.

Once both candles have fully burned down, clear away any sign of the spell and destroy the letter by safely burning it or ripping it up and throwing it away. Cleanse your hematite crystal by leaving it out in the moonlight for the next two nights when the moon is at its fullest.

The person or people who have set out to harm you will soon have that energy returned to them.

Protection Pendant Spell

PURPOSE

To secure daily protection

WHEN TO CAST

Any time on a Saturday during any moon phase

WHAT YOU NEED

3 drops each of lavender, peppermint and sandalwood essential oils

a pinch of salt

a small bowl

a pink tealight candle

your favourite necklace or pendant

a paper towel

Many witches will wear a pentagram necklace to protect them from any negative energy, but some people feel uncomfortable wearing something that represents witchcraft. With this spell, you can make any necklace your protection necklace. Saturday is the day associated with the planet Saturn and is the perfect day to cast protection spells.

WHAT TO DO

Combine all three essential oils in the bowl, then add the salt and mix together using the index finger on your right hand. With the oil on your finger, draw a circle around the top of the pink candle. Light the candle and imagine the heat from the flame reaching up and engulfing you with its protection.

Next, place the whole necklace into your oil mixture and swish it around for a minute or so. Continue to visualize the warm glow of the flame sending out protection to you.

Take the necklace out of the oil and wipe all the mixture from it. Make sure you clean it thoroughly so as not to tarnish any metal. Say the following words three times:

I CALL UPON Divine to protect this pendant of mine,
So mote it be.

Allow the candle to burn down safely and dispose of any remaining oil in the bin (not down the sink or toilet) Allow your necklace to dry. You can now wear it, knowing that you are protected every time you do so. You can do this spell with any item of jewellery – just substitute the word 'pendant' for the name of the item you wish to protect.

'Back Off Bully'
Spell

Purpose

To make a bully go away

When to Cast

Midnight on any day during any moon phase

What You Need

a black candle

cedarwood essential oil

a small piece of paper

a black pen

1 metre (1 yard) black cotton or thread

a needle

a bag of salt and vinegar crisps (potato chips)

a heatproof dish or cauldron

It's never fun when you are being bullied by someone, whether that be in school, at work or in your personal life. We're all aware that hurt people hurt people, and because of this, we often make allowances and let bullies get away with their unkind ways. But this is exhausting when you are the victim of a bully. Sometimes, the only thing to do is cast a karma spell to send the bully on their way. Make sure you cast this spell outside or somewhere away from flammable surroundings.

WHAT TO DO

You can perform this spell at any time of the month, so long as you cast it at midnight – the witching hour.

First, take your candle and rub the cedarwood oil into it, working from the bottom to the top. If you are using a tealight candle, simply add a few drops to it and rub it in. Gather all the other ingredients together on a table so that you have everything to hand.

Next, light the candle and, with your non-dominant hand, write the name of the person who has been bullying you on the piece of paper using the black pen. Visualize this person and all the harm they have done to you. Fold the piece of paper into a paper plane. Take the length of black cotton and thread it through the needle, then knot it at the end. Push the needle through the paper airplane you have made, so that it is hanging from the thread.

Open your bag of crisps, ready for the next part of the spell. Concentrate your mind on the candle flame as you hang the paper plane over it so it catches fire. Imagine you have the power to burn your bully out of your life for good. Hold the burning plane over the heatproof dish or cauldron to catch the ash, dropping the thread into the dish or cauldron if the thread catches light. Once the plane and thread have burned away, you will have a little pile of ash in your fireproof dish. Shake this into the bag of salt and vinegar crisps and close the bag again. Say the following words just once:

**GET OUT, GET OUT, GET OUT OF MY LIFE,
YOU WILL NEVER CAUSE ME FURTHER
STRIFE.**

**YOU ARE BANISHED TO NOW LEAVE ME BE
THIS SPELL IS BOUND FOR ETERNITY.**

SO MOTE IT BE.

As you say, 'So mote it be,' bang your fist down three times on the crisp packet, shattering the crisps inside. Do not open the packet again. Dispose of it in the trash, then blow out the candle to use again if you need to repeat this spell.

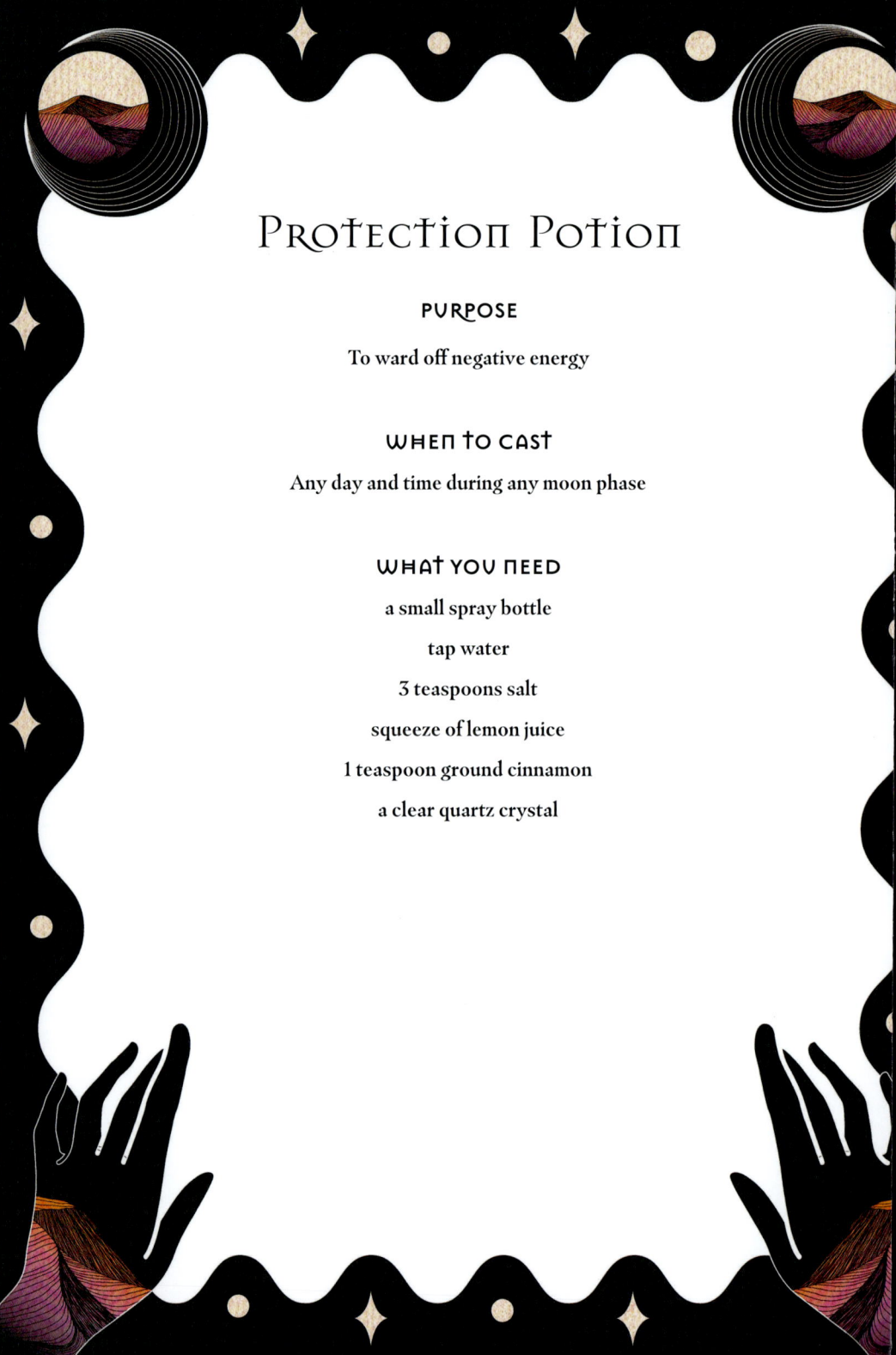

Protection Potion

PURPOSE

To ward off negative energy

WHEN TO CAST

Any day and time during any moon phase

WHAT YOU NEED

a small spray bottle

tap water

3 teaspoons salt

squeeze of lemon juice

1 teaspoon ground cinnamon

a clear quartz crystal

Have you ever noticed that when you're around certain people, your mood changes? It can be hard when you find yourself surrounded by negative people, and studies have shown that negative energy transfers from person to person quicker than positive energy. This is why it's so important to protect yourself on a regular basis. You can cast this spell any time you know you will be around energy-vampires.

WHAT TO DO

To prepare your protection potion, fill your spray bottle two-thirds of the way up with tap water. Add the salt, lemon juice and cinnamon, along with your clear quartz crystal. Place the lid on the bottle and shake until all the ingredients are mixed together.

When you go out and you feel you might bump into negative people, simply spritz yourself with a few sprays of your protection potion. Any negative comments or energy will be repelled.

Replace your potion weekly.

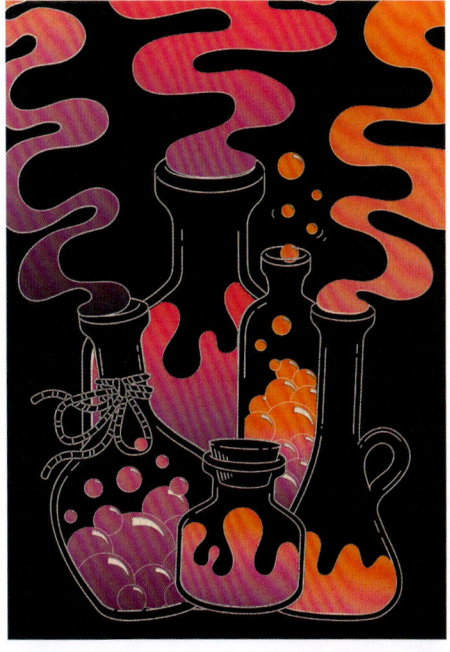

Spell To Banish Money Worries

PURPOSE
To alleviate financial anxiety

WHEN TO CAST
Any time on a Friday during any moon phase

WHAT YOU NEED

For part one

a clear glass tumbler | tap water

3 teaspoons salt | 3 teaspoons vinegar

a paper straw

For part two

a new glass tumbler | tap water

a paper straw | lemon juice

pinch of dried rosemary | pinch of dried mint

1 mint leaf

It's no fun worrying about money and how you're going to pay your bills. As any good witch will know, worrying will only manifest what you're worrying about. It's important to remember that money is just a commodity that we use as a means to exchange one thing for another. Because we are so used to using this commodity, it holds a lot of energy in our lives. This spell is one of those tried-and-tested ones that you can refer to whenever you find yourself facing money anxiety. It will help you concentrate on manifesting the amount of money you need. This spell is in two parts, so there are more ingredients than usual.

WHAT TO DO

Part one
The first part of the spell focuses on the blockages you may have around receiving money. You won't ever stop worrying about money unless you remove the energy that is blocking you.

Fill your glass tumbler halfway with ordinary tap water, then add the salt and vinegar to the water. Take the paper straw and mix the solution in an anticlockwise direction. As you do so, say the following words:

MONEY WORRIES, MONEY PROBLEMS, NO LONGER WILL YOU HAVE CONTROL OVER ME, NO LONGER WILL YOU BLIGHT MY LIFE.

I BANISH THE NEGATIVE ENERGY SURROUNDING MONEY.

FROM THIS DAY FORTH I CALL ON THE POWER OF BEL TO HELP IN MY QUEST.

SO MOTE IT BE.

Visualize all the negative energy surrounding money swirling backwards inside the glass tumbler as you continue to stir the solution. When you feel happy that the negative energy has all gone, stop stirring and allow the solution to settle again. Blow into the straw to create bubbles of your intention to stop worrying about money. Once the water has settled again, pour it down the toilet and flush it away. Dispose of the straw in your recycling bin.

Part two
Now that you've banished any worries surrounding money, the second part of the spell is to encourage more money to come your way. Again, it's important to remember that there is a lot of energy involved in the exchange of money. Once you finish this spell, you will notice more money coming to you in unexpected ways. Think of this part of the spell as your very own prosperity cocktail!

Fill your fresh glass halfway with tap water and begin stirring the water in a clockwise direction with the paper straw. As the water swirls around, slowly add a few squirts of lemon juice, followed by a pinch of dried rosemary and a pinch of dried mint. Keep stirring the potion in a clockwise direction for a few minutes while visualizing the energy of money coming to you.

Stop stirring and allow the mixture to stop spinning, then place the mint leaf on top and say the following words:

BY THE POWER OF LAKSHMI, I CALL UPON WEALTH AND ABUNDANCE TO NOW ENTER MY LIFE.

FROM THIS DAY, I WILL ATTRACT FORTUNE AND PROSPERITY

AND NEVER FEEL LACKING AGAIN.

SO MOTE IT BE.

Traditionally, witches would drink their prosperity cocktail, but it's fine if you just want to take a sip. Once again, blow your intention through the straw and into the potion. If you decide not to drink your potion, pour it on the ground outside your house to encourage wealth to bless your home. Dispose of the paper straw in your recycling bin. You should soon see an increase in wealth and prosperity.

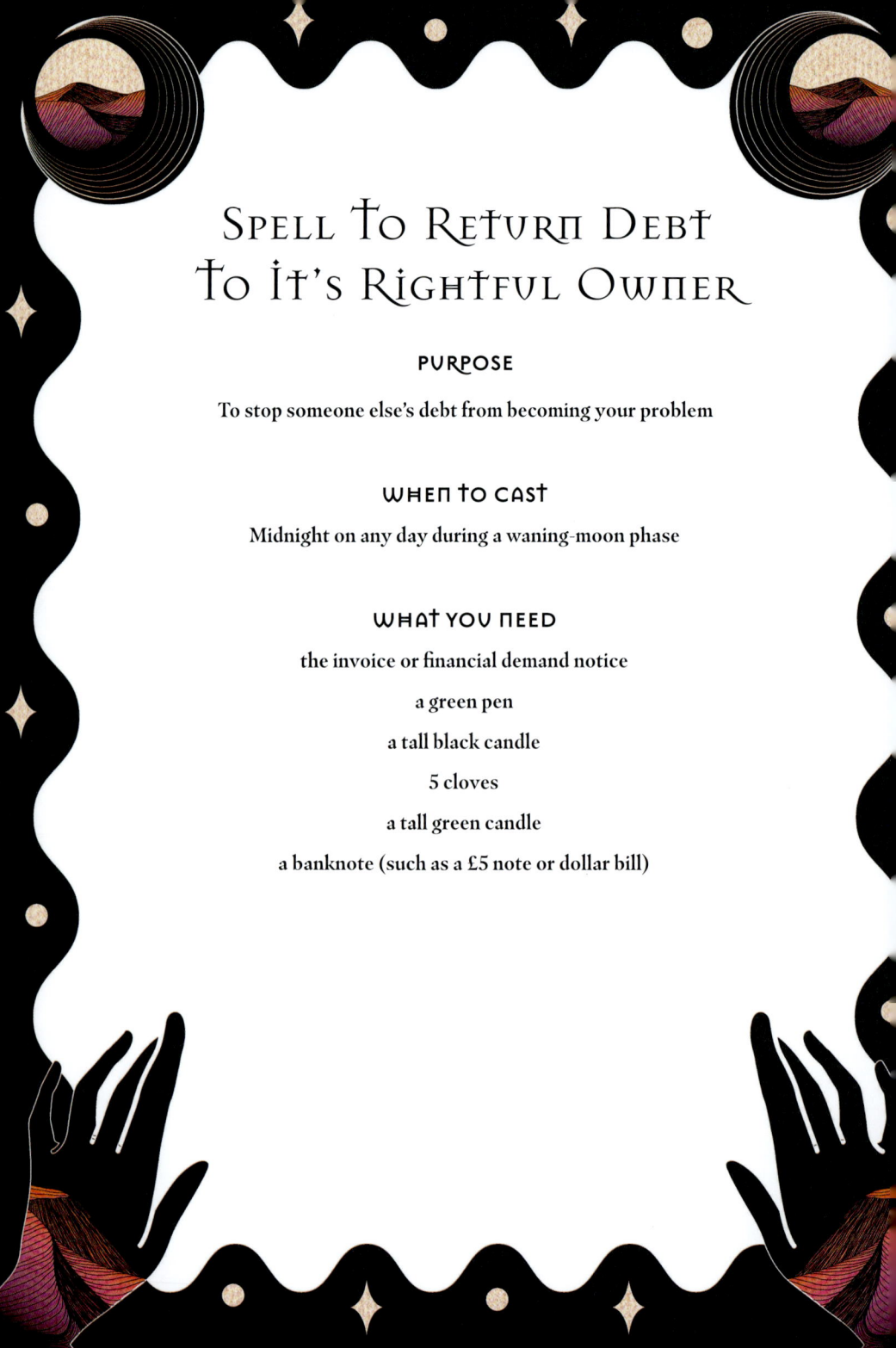

Spell To Return Debt To It's Rightful Owner

PURPOSE

To stop someone else's debt from becoming your problem

WHEN TO CAST

Midnight on any day during a waning-moon phase

WHAT YOU NEED

the invoice or financial demand notice

a green pen

a tall black candle

5 cloves

a tall green candle

a banknote (such as a £5 note or dollar bill)

When couples or friends split up or fall out, it can often result in one person taking on the other person's debts and being landed with a financial liability that isn't theirs. The most important thing to do is to contact whoever the debt is with and officially make a declaration that this is not your debt, but this spell will also ensure that you don't become obliged to pay for someone else's bad financial choices.

WHAT TO DO

Concentrate on the amount of money that is owed and imagine that you are physically pushing it away from you. On the demand notice or invoice, write 'Return to Sender' across the top in green pen. Place the demand notice or invoice underneath the black candle, then place the cloves on top of the paper. Light the candle and visualize the debt being returned to whoever is truly responsible for it.

Allow the candle to safely burn down, then screw up the invoice or demand, along with the cloves and any leftover wax residue. Throw it all into the bin.

Now place the green candle on top of your paper money. Light the candle and imagine being free of this debt that doesn't belong to you. Allow the candle to safely burn away. If there is any wax left over, roll it into a small ball, allow it to cool and keep it in your wallet or purse until the situation is resolved.

Justice will prevail and you will no longer be responsible for a debt that was never yours.

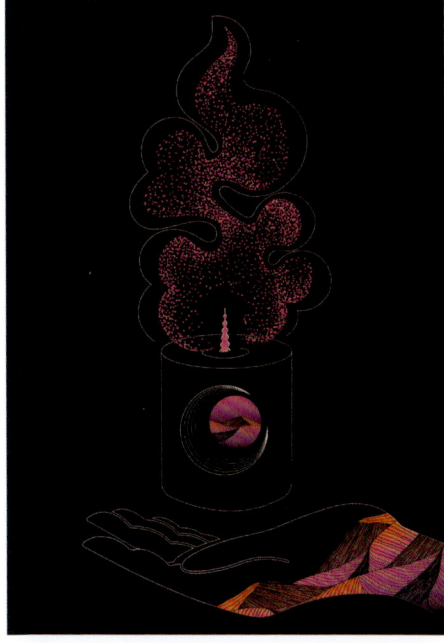

'Just My Luck' Spell

PURPOSE

To bring good luck back to you

WHEN TO CAST

Any day and time during any moon phase

WHAT YOU NEED

boiling water

a peppermint teabag

your favourite cup

1 teaspoon honey

a pinch of ground ginger

a pinch of ground cinnamon

a pinch of ground nutmeg

a drop of lemon juice

a teaspoon

a tiger's eye crystal

If you're having a run of bad luck, it doesn't necessarily mean that you've been cursed or that you're being punished by the karma gods; sometimes luck is simply not on your side, and sometimes challenges are sent to all of us so that we learn lessons. Regardless, if you've noticed that things simply aren't going your way right now, this lovely little spell will bring back your good luck.

WHAT TO DO

Traditionally, witches would boil water over a fire or on the stove, so if you can, do this. If you can't, simply boil a kettle. Place your peppermint teabag into your favourite cup and pour over the water. Allow it to brew for a few minutes, then remove the teabag. Add the honey, spices and lemon juice one by one, and imagine your luck increasing as you add each ingredient to the cup. Stir with a teaspoon. Now add the tiger's eye crystal and allow it to remain in the cup for three minutes (if you prefer, you can just place the crystal next to the cup).

Scoop out the tiger's eye and leave it to dry on some kitchen paper. Stir your magic tea in a clockwise direction three times. Cup the tea in your hands and sip it as you visualize your luck improving. It's important not to dwell on any bad luck or misfortune you've encountered, and instead to focus your mind on your future and how lucky you are going to be now.

When you've finished your tea, turn your cup upside down and turn it in a clockwise direction three times to complete the spell.

Keep your tiger's eye crystal on you to keep the good luck coming to you.

Power Neutralizer Spell

PURPOSE

To rebalance power dynamics

WHEN TO CAST

Any day and time during any moon phase

WHAT YOU NEED

a spray bottle

5 drops each of eucalyptus oil, peppermint oil and lavender oil

tap water

a paper towel

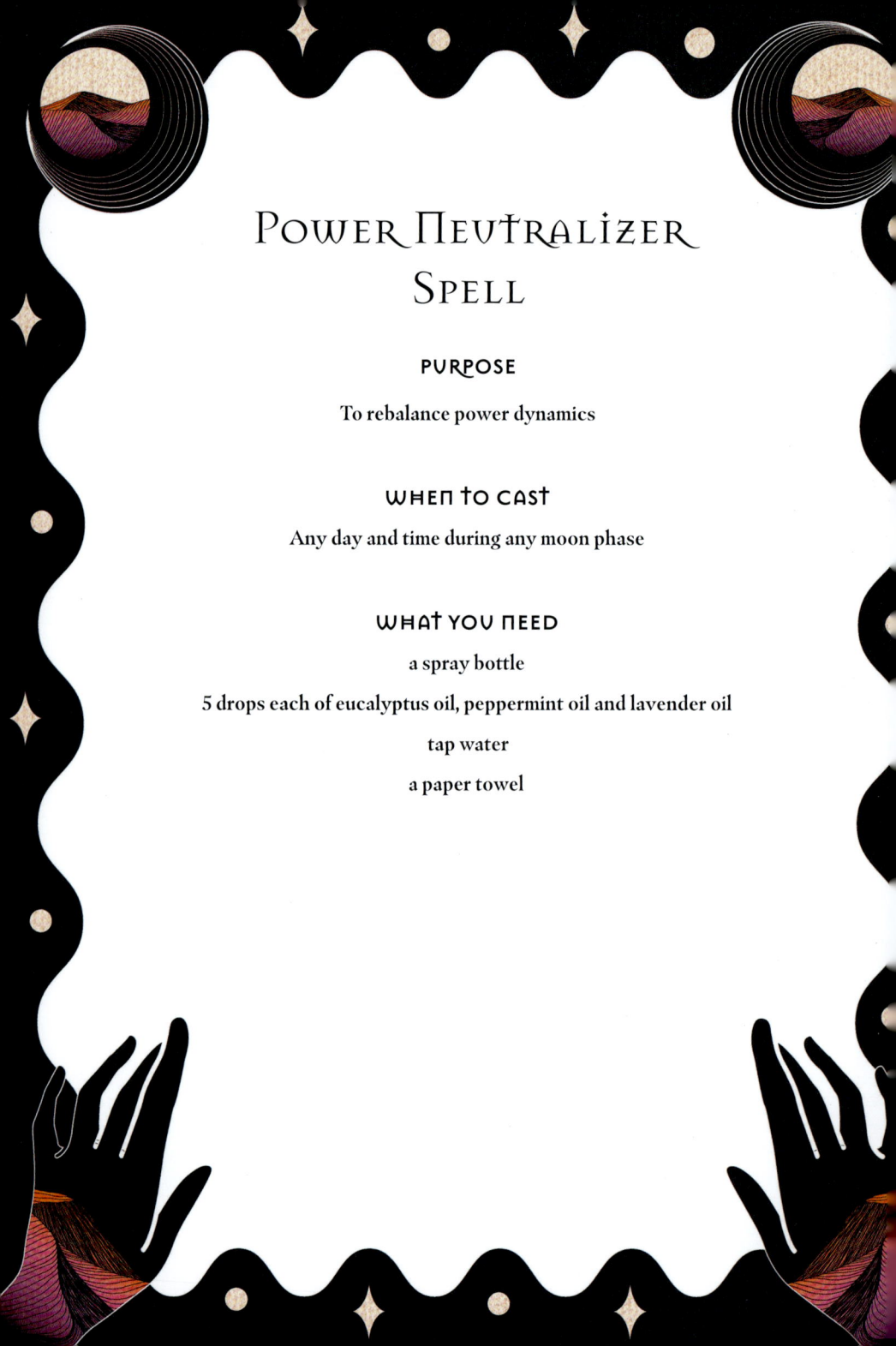

You can sometimes find yourself in a situation where your power has quietly been taken away from you. People who abuse their power are not necessarily narcissists. Sometimes, it's just that they've let power and authority go to their heads. If you feel that a relationship has become unbalanced in some way, try this little spell to neutralize the uneven balance of power.

WHAT TO DO

Fill your spray bottle almost to the top with ordinary tap water. Add the eucalyptus, peppermint and lavender oils to the water, and give the bottle a good shake. As you do so, visualize the liquid mixing together to create a magic formula.

Turn the nozzle to 'spray' rather than 'squirt', if your bottle has the option. Stand up tall and say three times:

I AM A WARRIOR AND I TAKE BACK MY POWER!

As you do this, spray the potion high into the air and walk through the mist as it falls to the ground. Repeat this action three times, then turn clockwise in a full circle and say:

THE SPELL IS CAST.

Your power will now be restored, and you will be a match to anyone who tries to undermine you or abuse their authority over you. Your powerful potion will keep for three months, so anytime you feel that someone is taking your power from you, give yourself a little power spritz.

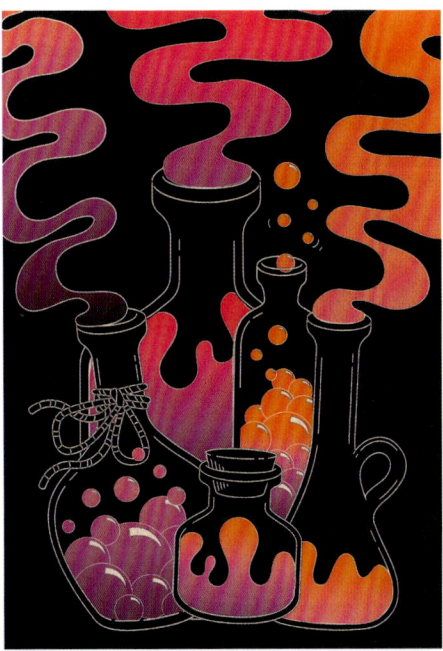

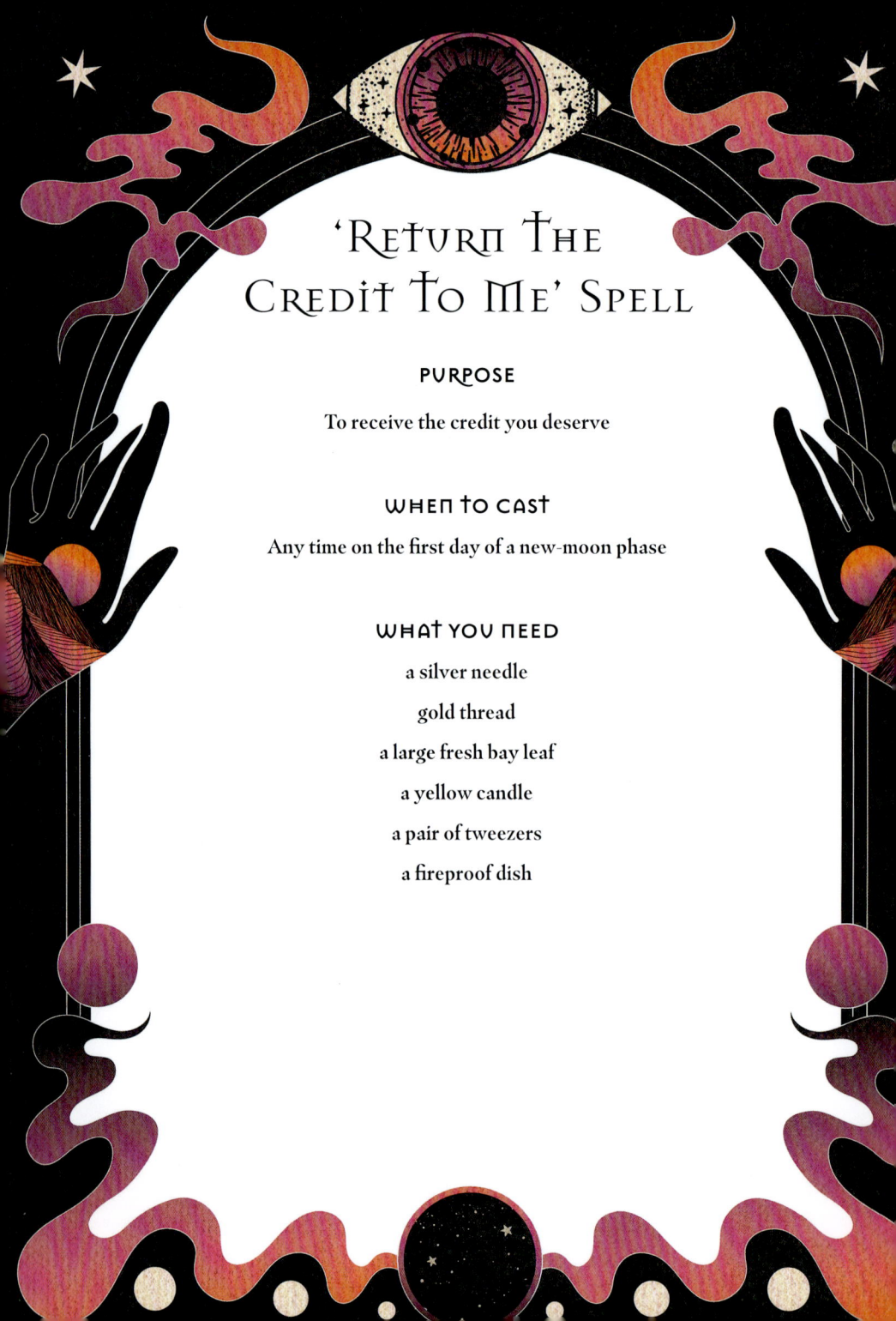

'Return The Credit To Me' Spell

PURPOSE

To receive the credit you deserve

WHEN TO CAST

Any time on the first day of a new-moon phase

WHAT YOU NEED

a silver needle

gold thread

a large fresh bay leaf

a yellow candle

a pair of tweezers

a fireproof dish

Imagine the situation: you've worked hard on a project or helped someone out in some way, and then someone else comes along and ends up taking the credit for it. Annoying, isn't it? Unfortunately, there are some people in the world who will use you and your talents or work and pass them off as their own. This spell will ensure that the truth comes out, and you will receive the credit you deserve.

WHAT TO DO

Think of the person who has stolen or taken advantage of your ideas or work and passed off your efforts as their own. Thread your needle with the gold thread and carefully embroider their initials into the bay leaf. Always use a fresh bay leaf, because dried ones are prone to breaking when you try to sew them.

Light your yellow candle and look into the flame. Say the following words:

BY THE POWER OF BRIDGID, I COMMAND THAT YOU RETURN WHAT IS NOT YOURS.

BY THE POWER OF BRIDGID, I COMMAND THAT YOU SURRENDER ALL CREDIT,

WHICH WE BOTH KNOW IS MINE AND MINE ALONE.
THIS IS MY DEMAND,

SO MOTE IT BE.

Visualize the goddess Bridgid coming to your aid and fighting for justice and fairness for you, and imagine the perpetrator finally being exposed as the thief of your work or ideas.

Place the bay leaf into the flame using the tweezers, and once it's alight, hold it over your fireproof dish and watch it burn – it might crackle a bit due to the moisture in the leaf. Once it has burned away, you can blow out the candle for use another day.

The person who took the credit from you will soon be exposed.

'The Law Is On My Side' Spell

PURPOSE

To help you deal with legal matters

WHEN TO CAST

Any day and time during a full-moon phase

WHAT YOU NEED

a picture of the Justice Tarot card (you can find one on the internet and print it out rather than cutting up a real Tarot card)

a pair of scissors

a pestle and mortar (or a bowl and spoon)

a pinch of dried rosemary

a pinch of dried basil

eggshell of one hen's egg

a heatproof dish or cauldron

It can be quite frightening when you are faced with a court summons or subpoena, and you are completely innocent. The most important thing is to make sure that you or your legal team have all your evidence prepared in advance and that you remain calm and collected. This justice karma spell will help you to win your case, or have you exonerated by the judge or legal system.

WHAT TO DO

Take the picture of the Justice Tarot card and use the scissors to cut it up into tiny pieces, as small as you can make them. Put the contents into your mortar or bowl. Add the herbs and the eggshell, then use your pestle or the back of a spoon to grind everything together as finely as possible. As you do this, say the following words:

I CALL UPON HECATE TO HEAR MY PLEA:

BRING JUSTICE HERE TO ME.

RIGHT THE WRONGS THAT HAVE BEEN DONE,
EXONERATE ME, OH MIGHTY ONE.

SEND MISFORTUNE BACK TO THOSE
RESPONSIBLE FOR MY CURRENT WOES.

SEND KARMIC DEBT
SO THAT THEY WILL NEVER FORGET.

HEAR MY PLEA AND BRING JUSTICE BACK TO ME,
SO IT WILL BE.

When you are happy that your ingredients are as finely ground as you can get them, pop them into a little zip-lock bag or envelope and take them with you to the court.

Sprinkle half of the package outside the court and the other half inside the court. If this isn't possible, place a pinch of the ground ingredients into each of your shoes before going into court.

You should have justice returned to you.

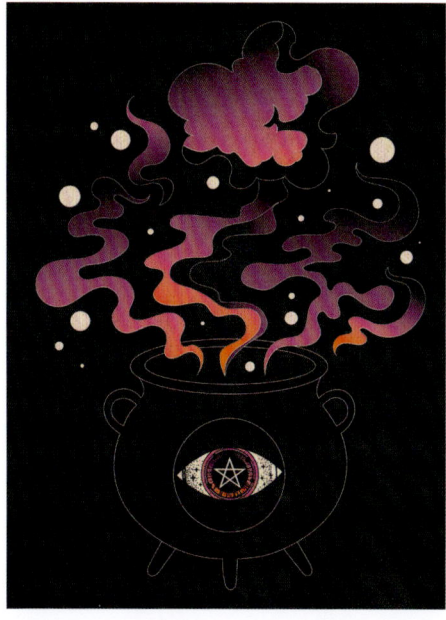

Spell To Find Your Dream Job

PURPOSE

To find a job you really love

WHEN TO CAST

Any day and time on the night of a full moon

WHAT YOU NEED

a computer and printer

a piece of paper

a handful of ground cinnamon

an envelope

a pen

Given that most of us have to work well into our old age, it makes sense to find something that you love but also pays you enough to live your life. This spell will help you to find a job that you love doing, whether that's working for someone else or working for yourself.

WHAT TO DO

Remember, magic and spellcasting is as much about intention as it is about the equipment you use, so for this reason you need to get yourself into a positive mindset when finding your dream job.

Go online and search for any images that represent your ideal job. Copy and paste these images into a new printable document, along with words affirming your new job. For example, if you want to start a floristry business, find images that relate to what looks like your dream workplace. If there is a particular company you've always wanted to work at, use a picture of their headquarters, logo or CEO. Add your ideal hours and salary into your document. Spend a little time on this, because while you may want a huge salary, that may also come at a cost to your free time, so always ensure that you are very specific with what you really want. Once you are happy with what you require, print out the page you've created.

Look at what you've printed out and visualize being called in for an interview or receiving an email from the bank telling you they have offered you a business loan for your start-up idea. Really feel as though it is happening right now. You'll know this is working when you get a little feeling of excitement and hope.

Next, place a handful of ground cinnamon in your dominant hand and blow it on to your dream job manifestation page. Say the following words:

**BY THE POWER OF THREE,
I SEND MY REQUEST OUT TO THE UNIVERSE.**

**BY THE POWER OF THREE,
MY DREAM JOB COMES TO ME.**

SO IT BE.

Fold the cinnamon-covered paper into three and place it in the envelope. Seal it, then write today's date on the envelope, along with the words 'dream job'. Leave this under your pillow until the next full moon. You should find that opportunities seem to come to you like magic within the month.

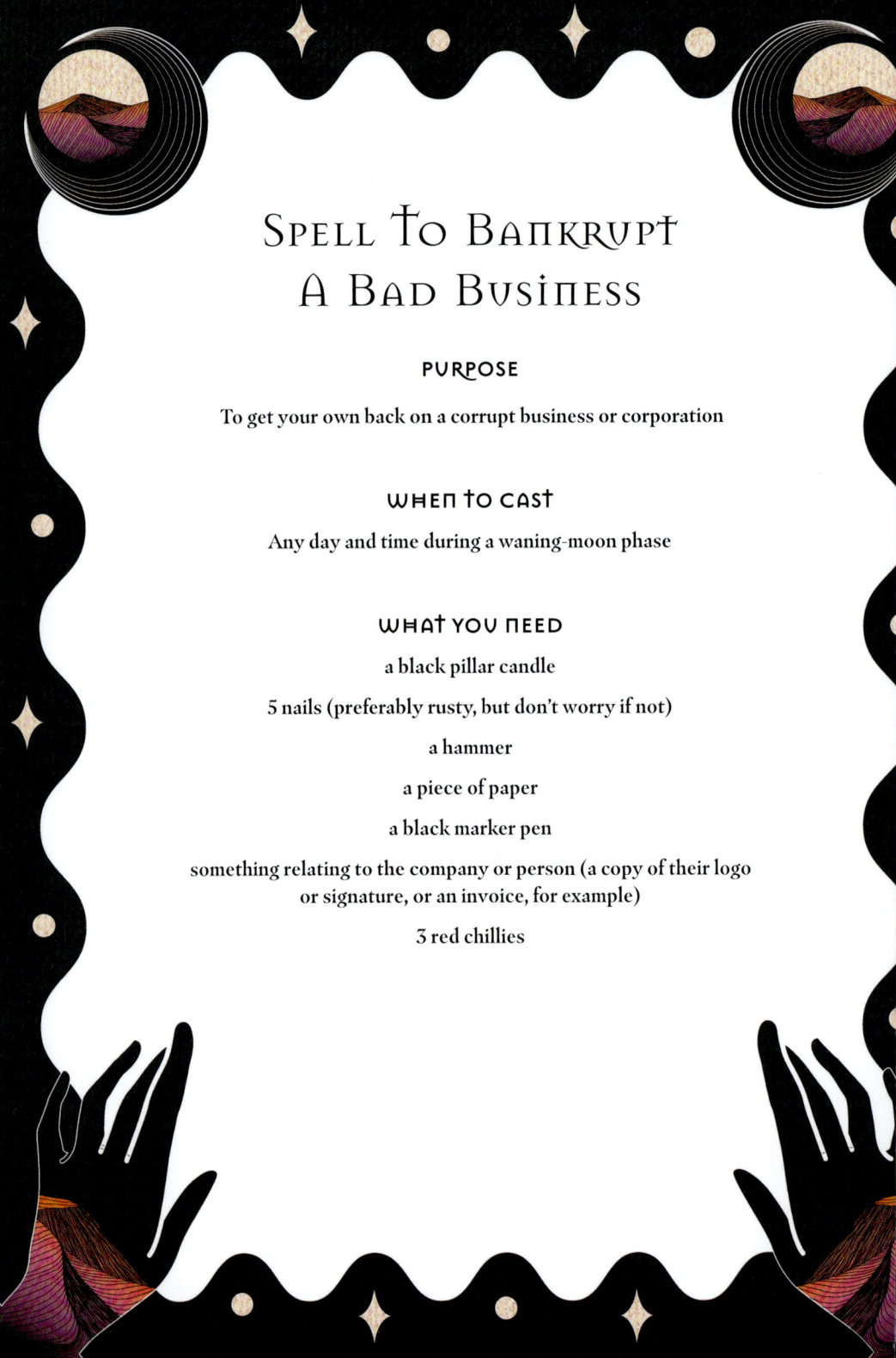

Spell To Bankrupt
A Bad Business

PURPOSE

To get your own back on a corrupt business or corporation

WHEN TO CAST

Any day and time during a waning-moon phase

WHAT YOU NEED

a black pillar candle

5 nails (preferably rusty, but don't worry if not)

a hammer

a piece of paper

a black marker pen

something relating to the company or person (a copy of their logo
or signature, or an invoice, for example)

3 red chillies

Unfortunately, there are some unscrupulous and greedy people in the world who run businesses, care little for their customers and feel that they have the power to abuse their positions. Fortunately, though, the laws of karma apply to everyone. Mix this with a little magic and you can be assured that that cowboy builder or that devious business associate will lose their customers and their business for good. This is a very powerful spell, and I have seen it work many times.

WHAT TO DO

If you feel angry at being mistreated, then this is the time to allow that anger to come out, because this will give your spell more power! First of all, place your candle on its side, on a firm surface. Hold it securely in place so that it doesn't roll around, and, working in a line going down the candle, carefully hammer the five nails into it. As you do this, imagine that the universe is conspiring with you to dish out justice to this company or person.

Stand the candle upright again and place to one side. Next, draw a large pentagram symbol in the middle of the piece of paper. On top of the pentagram, place the item relating to the company, business or person, then finally place the black candle on top. Take the red chillies and arrange them around the base of the candle so that they form a triangle shape.

Light your candle and repeat the following three times:

[NAME OF PERSON/BUSINESS], YOUR ACTIONS HAVE DESTROYED MANY.

YOU HAVE BEEN DECEITFUL FOR THE PENNY.

NO LONGER WILL YOU PROJECT DECEPTION.

OF THIS I'M CERTAIN, THIS IS MY MISSION.

YOU WILL NO LONGER BE ABLE TO OPERATE, YOU HAVE NOW SEALED YOUR OWN FATE.

SO MOTE IT BE.

As the candle burns down and the nails fall out, you should start feeling more empowered with the belief that this person, business or company will no longer be able to deceive others.

Allow the candle to safely burn down. Collect the nails, any wax residue and the chillies and scrunch it all up in the paper. Dispose of this in an outside bin. This spell often takes a while to manifest, but it will manifest.

Academic Ascension Spell

PURPOSE

To boost your grades

WHEN TO CAST

Any day and time during a new-moon phase

WHAT YOU NEED

a lavender incense stick and holder

your textbook or study guide

an orange candle

a yellow candle

a piece of yellow paper

a pen

People assume that within the laws of karma, it is written that if you do good and work hard enough, everything will land in your lap. As I pointed out earlier in the book, karma isn't quite as simple as that. Sometimes it needs a little push in the right direction. You can study a subject for hours on end, but sometimes it's still not enough. Sometimes what you've learned just goes out of your head again, and this can be for a number of reasons, such as being distracted by something else, or a deep-seated belief that you're not capable.

By casting this spell prior to an exam or test, you will be better prepared to succeed.

WHAT TO DO

Light the incense stick and blow it out so that the smoke drifts into the air. Draw a circle of serenity around yourself with the incense stick, then wave the stick over your textbook or study guide. The incense will calm you and get you in the right frame of mind to perform this spell.

Place the incense stick in a holder. Next, light the two candles side by side. On your piece of yellow paper, draw a picture of the sun. Visualize the energy of the sun warming you and giving you that feeling of peace and tranquillity. Repeat the following words three times:

I INVOKE THE POWER OF THE SUN
FOR HELP WITH THIS PROBLEM.

I NOW HAVE THE CONFIDENCE REQUIRED
TO PASS WITH FLYING COLOURS.

SO MOTE IT BE.

Spend a few minutes visualizing and feeling how it will feel to have passed your test or exam, and really believe that it is possible.

Blow out the candles (which you can use again if needed). When you take your test or exam, take the piece of paper you drew the sun on with you as your lucky charm.

Spell To Banish Imposter Syndrome

PURPOSE

To get rid of your self-doubt

WHEN TO CAST

Any day and time during any moon phase

WHAT YOU NEED

lavender essential oil

3 white tealight candles

a notebook

a pen

Everyone experiences self-doubt and imposter syndrome from time to time, and it's important to remember that even the most confident people question whether they are good enough. This little spell will help you remember that you are deserving of the opportunities before you.

WHAT TO DO

Find a quiet place to sit for 10 minutes. Place one drop of the lavender essential oil on to each tealight candle, then put one drop on each of your wrists, inner elbow joints and temples. Breathe deeply for the count of three and exhale.

Take your notebook and pen and write down what it is that you think you're not good enough at, and why you're worried that other people will think that you're an imposter. By writing down your thoughts into words, you can dispel them from your mind.

Light the three candles and set your focus on the three flames. Keep taking deep breaths. Say out loud 13 times:

Nam-myoho-renge-kyo,
I am worthy, I am me!

After each sentence, take a deep breath in, hold for three and exhale again. You should feel a lot more relaxed at this point.

Re-read what you have written down in your notebook and remind yourself that these are just your thoughts; they're not real life. Now rip the page out of the notebook and shred the piece of paper, then throw it into the bin. Blow out the candles and breathe deeply again. You will be feeling a lot calmer now and can get on with your day without worrying.

Accountability Spell

PURPOSE

To make someone take accountability

WHEN TO CAST

Any day and time during a new-moon phase

WHAT YOU NEED

a pen belonging to the other person

a white tealight candle

a piece of paper

1 bay leaf

a heatproof dish or cauldron

Isn't it annoying and frustrating when someone refuses to take ownership of their behaviour? Whether it's a family member who refuses to accept responsibility for hurting you, or a work colleague who threw you under the bus when the fault was in fact their own, this karma spell makes another person take accountability for their actions, and will show others their true colours.

WHAT TO DO

Ask the person in question if you can borrow their pen, or just borrow it from their desk when they're not looking. Light the white tealight candle for self-protection and take out your piece of paper. Across the top, write the word: 'SORRY.' Now write as if you were the other person and were told that you had to write lines as a punishment for refusing to take accountability and for passing the buck.

If, for example, it was your boss who threw you under the bus at a board meeting, write something along the lines of: 'I apologize, [name], for taking your ideas and passing them off as my own.'

Write this line over and over again until the page is full, then turn the paper over and continue until that page is full, too.

On the bay leaf, write the initials of the offender in very small writing. Hold the paper to the candle until it catches fire, then carefully drop it into the heatproof dish or cauldron to burn safely. Once the ashes are cool, dispose of them in the bin.

When you next see the other person again, you need to return their pen to them and drop the bay leaf somewhere in their vicinity without them noticing.

You should soon receive an apology, or alternatively the offender's actions will be revealed to other people and they will be held accountable.

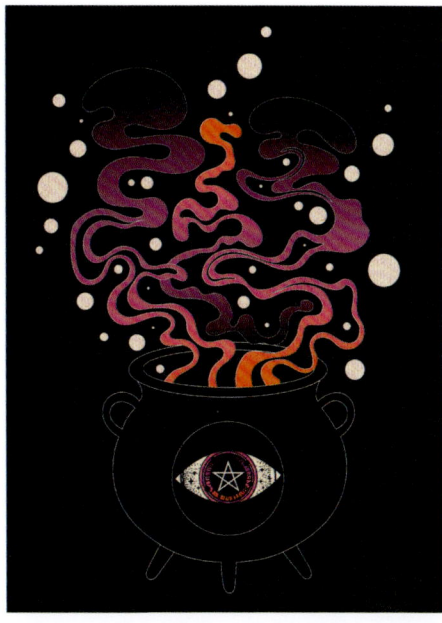

'Remotivate Me'
Spell

PURPOSE

To reignite your passion and drive

WHEN TO CAST

Any time on a Monday during any moon phase

WHAT YOU NEED

lemon juice

a small bowl

a cocktail stick

a small piece of paper, roughly 5cm (2in) square

a herb bundle (see page 36)

a fireproof plate

Sometimes it's hard to keep motivated with something that you know is good for you in the long run. For example, you know that exercise and working out regularly in the gym is good for you, but after that initial excitement, your interest can wain and you can find it a struggle to keep it up. Or you might know that studying for the next four years will mean that you will be in a better position to find the job you want, but it can get draining having to spend night after night studying rather than going out with your friends. This little spell will help you to get motivated again – and remember, as with the laws of karma, what you put out will come back to you aplenty.

WHAT TO DO

Pour some lemon juice into a small bowl and get your piece of paper ready. You're going to use your cocktail stick like a pen. Dip the cocktail stick into the lemon juice and then write what it is you wish to have more motivation for. This could be the word 'gym', or 'study', or 'housework', or just 'life' in general. Keep dipping the cocktail stick into the lemon juice until you have written what you want to write.

Allow the lemon juice to dry, and then roll up the piece of paper into a tight scroll. You will need to loosen your herb bundle a little, because you need to push the scroll into the top centre of the bundle. When you have done this, tighten the string around the bundle. Now you are ready to remotivate yourself.

Light your herb bundle and blow out any flames. It should now be smouldering and giving off smoke. Starting at your head, waft the smoke in a clockwise motion around your head, neck, shoulders, upper body, arms, tummy, legs and finally down to your feet.

As you do so, repeat the following words 13 times:

Motivus restituere repeto

(*These words are Latin for: 'To seek and restore motive'.*)

When you've finished, leave the herb bundle to continue smouldering on a fireproof plate. The spell will have been cast once the bundle stops producing smoke on its own.

The paper you put inside should have burned away, but if it hasn't and the herb bundle has gone out, you can take the piece of paper out again with a pair of tweezers and throw it away. You can then reuse your herb bundle for another spell. Alternatively, you can keep this herb bundle purely for motivation spells in the future.

Within 24 hours, you should be feeling more motivated to achieve your life goals again.

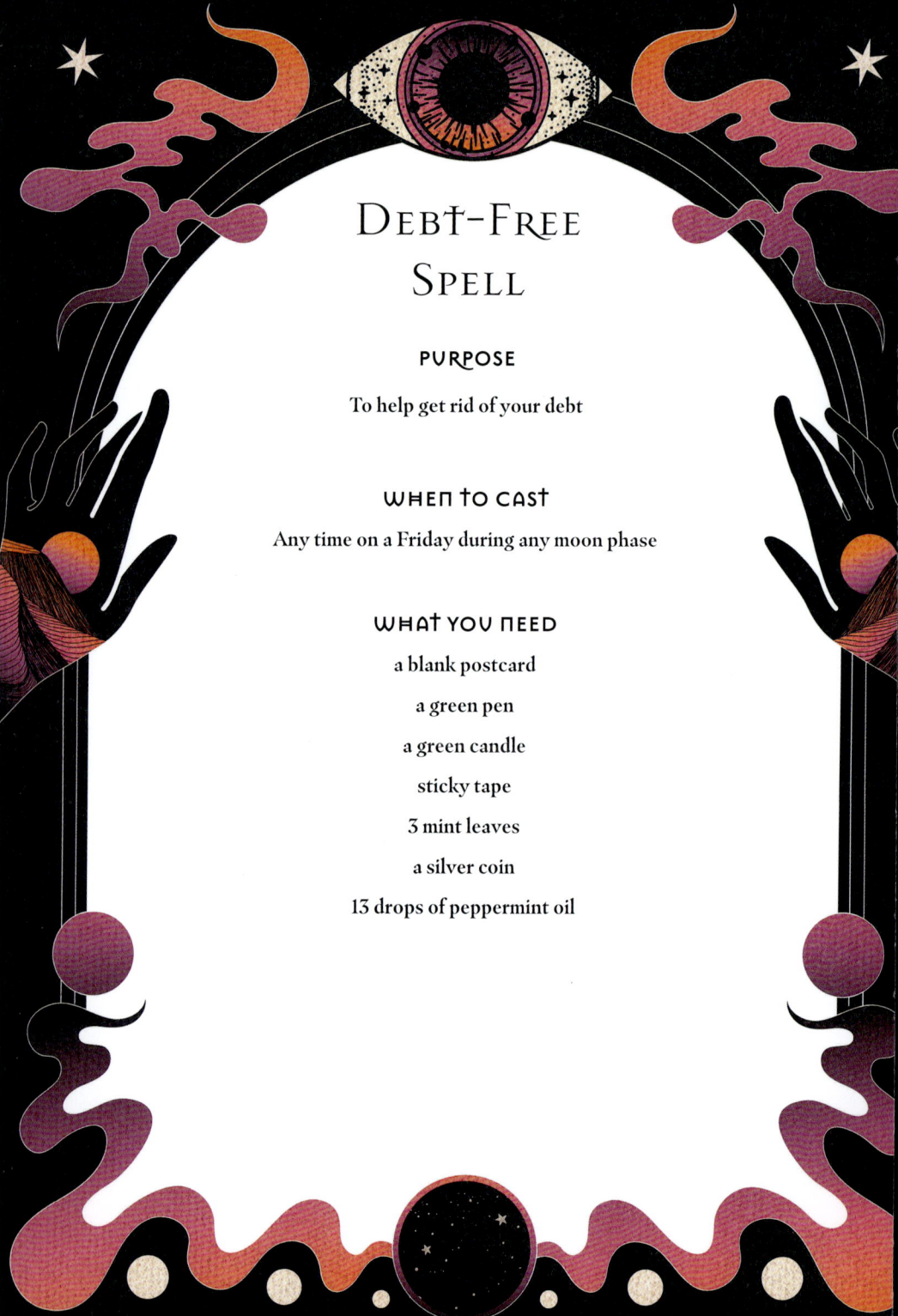

Debt-Free Spell

PURPOSE

To help get rid of your debt

WHEN TO CAST

Any time on a Friday during any moon phase

WHAT YOU NEED

a blank postcard

a green pen

a green candle

sticky tape

3 mint leaves

a silver coin

13 drops of peppermint oil

It's important to remember that money is just an exchange commodity which we use every day in exchange for goods, services or products. While nobody can live without money, it doesn't have to be the be-all and end-all in life. Here is an easy spell to fast-track your way to becoming debt-free.

WHAT TO DO

Find a time when you can sit quietly and write. On the postcard, use your green pen to write down exactly how much you owe and to whom (use both sides of the postcard if necessary). When you've finished, light the green candle, then tape the mint leaves and silver coin to the postcard.

Drop 13 drops of peppermint oil on to the postcard and say the following phrase 13 times:

Allow the candle to burn away and dispose of any leftover wax in the bin. Place the postcard either under your bed or under your pillow for the next 28 days. You will see more money coming your way, or debts being settled, by the end of the month.

**MONEY LORD, HEAR MY PLEA,
LOOK MY WAY, LOOK MY WAY.**

BRING YOUR ABUNDANCE TO ME.

I GIVE THANKS

'Back On Track'
Spell

PURPOSE

To help you achieve your goals

WHEN TO CAST

Any day and time during a new-moon phase

WHAT YOU NEED

1 teaspoon yarrow (ground or dried leaves; available at most good health stores)

2 bay leaves

3 mint leaves

1 teaspoon dried lavender

a pestle and mortar (or a bowl and spoon)

Sometimes life events can get in the way of you being the best version of yourself, and the smallest of things can have a big impact on things like your grades, deadlines or whether you're considered for a promotion. If you've been having a hard time and it's been affecting your ability to get ahead, do this simple, empowering spell to get yourself back on track.

WHAT TO DO

Combine the yarrow, bay leaves, mint leaves and lavender in your mortar or bowl and grind them up using the pestle or the back of a spoon until they become a fine powder. As you do so, visualize yourself being the best at what you do, and realizing that this difficult time has just been a small blip.

Once you have ground your ingredients into powder form, say the following words:

NEW moon, new moon,
I call upon thee
To bring back the best version of me.

NEW moon, new moon,
On this day I decree
That you bring back my energy.

So mote it be.

When you have finished, take the powder to the room where you study or spend most of your time. Stand at the doorway and gently blow the powder into the room.

You will soon see your grades or your life in general improve.

Bad Boss Spell

PURPOSE

To help you deal with an awful boss

WHEN TO CAST

Any time on a Monday during any moon phase

WHAT YOU NEED

a black eyeliner

3 sheets of toilet paper

a cactus plant

a pair of tweezers

As we mentioned at the beginning of the book, people create their own karma, and you'll tend to find that difficult people who are hard to work with are suffering in some way. As the saying goes, hurt people hurt people. It's not your job to dish out bad karma to someone who is incapable of being pleasant to work with; they will eventually reap what they sow. What you can control is your own reaction to their bad behaviour – and you can do this with a little bit of magic.

WHAT TO DO

You need to prepare this spell prior to going in to work on a Monday (or whatever day is your first day back to work). With your eyeliner, draw the infinity symbol (like a number 8 turned on its side) on the middle piece of toilet paper, then draw a cross through it.

Next, carefully take one spike from the cactus plant with your tweezers and place the spike on top of the infinity symbol. Fold the two sides of toilet paper into the centre and say the following words:

A leader you are not,
And you need to learn a lesson
in treating people right.

You will change your ways
To become a nicer boss
Overnight.

Take your parcel with you in to work and find the bathroom that your boss uses, then flush the toilet-paper parcel down the toilet. You should see a difference in your boss's attitude within a day or two.

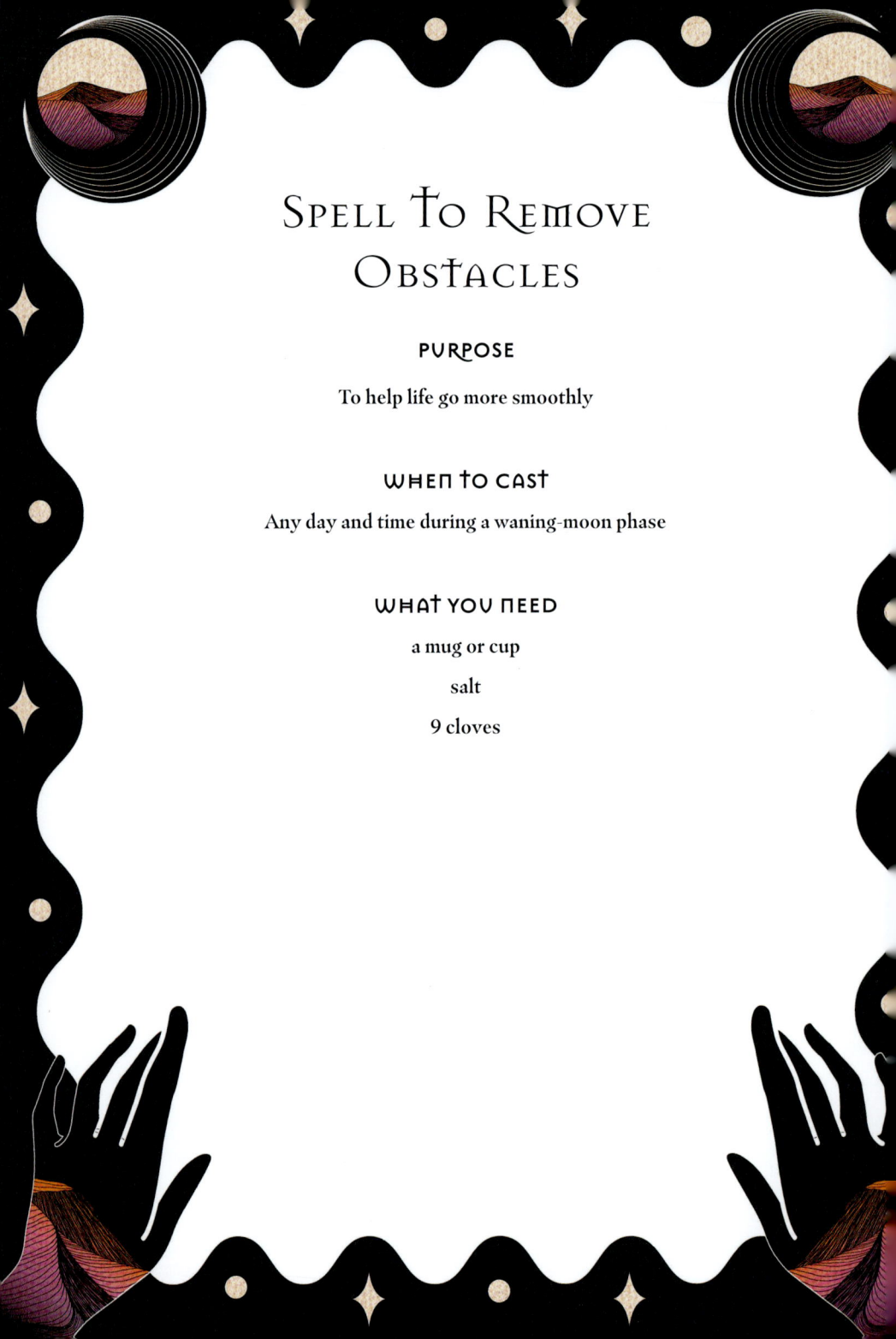

Spell To Remove Obstacles

PURPOSE

To help life go more smoothly

WHEN TO CAST

Any day and time during a waning-moon phase

WHAT YOU NEED

a mug or cup

salt

9 cloves

Cloves and salt have been used in spells for hundreds of years to help banish obstacles. Maybe you are in the process of buying a property and the transaction has been held up for some reason, or perhaps you are waiting for someone to make a decision before you can proceed with something. This easy spell will help to dissolve any obstacles in your path.

WHAT TO DO

On the first night of a waning moon, half-fill your cup or mug with salt. Place the cloves on told of the salt and say the following words:

BY THE POWER OF NINE.
I ASK THE DIVINE
TO REMOVE THESE OBSTACLES FROM MY
LIFE.

BY THE POWER OF NINE,
I ASK THE DIVINE
TO BRING FORTH ONLY PEACE AND SERENITY
TO ME.

BY THE POWER OF NINE,
I ASK THE DIVINE
TO JUMP OVER ANY OBSTACLES
THAT ARE HOLDING ME BACK.

SO MOTE IT BE.

Keep the mug or cup under your bed for the next 28 days. You should see any obstacles melt away within the month.

Two Choices Spell

PURPOSE

To help you make a tough decision

WHEN TO CAST

Any day and time during a full-moon phase

WHAT YOU NEED

2 tall white candles

2 silver sewing pins

2 small plates

2 small pieces of paper

a black pen

Sometimes you might find yourself faced with two equally appealing choices. Should you go on that holiday, or stay home? Should you apply for a new job or stay in your current position? Are you torn between two potential love matches? This simple decision spell will help you make the right choice.

WHAT TO DO

Find a spot where your candles won't be disturbed, because they need to be able to burn down. About halfway down each candle, push a silver sewing pin horizontally halfway through the shaft. Heat the base of each candle to enable it to stick to the plates (one candle per plate). On the first piece of paper, with your black pen, write down what one of your choices might be – for example, 'apply for a new job'. On the second piece of paper, write down the second options – for example, 'stay at my current job'.

Place the first piece of paper underneath the plate of one candle, and the second piece of paper under the second plate. This is the tricky part – try to light both candles at the same time. You might need to get a friend to help you with this.

Now you wait until the pin from one candle falls on to the plate. Look underneath that plate, and that will be your answer. It's important to examine how you feel when you receive your decision. If you feel disheartened at the outcome, then you truly knew what choice to make.

Spell To Help With a House Sale

PURPOSE

To make the selling process easier

WHEN TO CAST

Any time on a Friday during any moon phase

WHAT YOU NEED

3 mint plants in pots

peppermint essential oil

copy of your property details from your estate agent/realtor

a green marker pen

a green candle and a candle holder

Selling a house comes with all sorts of problems, whether it's finding a buyer who's not stuck in a chain or the anxiety you feel waiting for the solicitors to get all the legal paperwork completed. This little spell will help to accelerate the process and make it go more smoothly.

WHAT TO DO

Mint is associated with prosperity and success, so place two of the mint plants outside the front of your house or front door, and place the third in the back garden or at the back of your home. To encourage a buyer to feel interested in buying your property, sprinkle a few drops of peppermint essential oil on the doormat, or as close to the door as you can.

Take the copy of your property details and write the word 'SOLD' at the top with your green marker. Put it on a table or desk where it won't be disturbed.

Place the green candle in a candle holder and place this on top of the paperwork. Light the candle and say the following words:

HERE THEY COME, HERE THEY COME
THE RIGHT PERSON WHO LOVES MY HOME.

BY THE POWER OF THREE
MY HOUSE IS SOLD, SO MOTE IT BE.

Blow out the candle after saying these words. Every day for the next 28 days, repeat the rituals above, sprinkling the doormat with peppermint oil, then lighting the candle and repeating the words. You will have lots of interest in your property and it will sell quickly.

Spell To Banish Naughty Neighbours

PURPOSE

To make a bad neighbour move away

WHEN TO CAST

Any day and time during a waning-moon phase

WHAT YOU NEED

5 tall black candles | a tall orange candle

a black tourmaline crystal | a piece of paper

a black pen | a fireproof dish or cauldron

an envelope

Unfortunately, we can't choose who lives next door to us, but even the neighbours from hell can't escape the powers of witchcraft. Here is a powerful spell to banish them from your life.

WHAT TO DO

Gather all your ingredients on a table where they won't be disturbed, because this spell requires three days of spellcasting. Place the orange candle in the middle, then place the black candles in a circle around it. Place the black tourmaline in front of the orange candle. Black tourmaline is known for its powerful 'back off' energies, so it's the perfect crystal for this spell.

On day one, light the orange candle first – this represents your peace and protection. Then light all five black candles, lighting them in a clockwise direction.

Now sit for a while and contemplate all the trouble your neighbour has caused you, whether it's playing their music too loudly, calling you names over the fence or just being bad neighbours in general. Next, divide your paper into three sections by drawing two lines across the page. In the top section on your piece of paper, draw your neighbour's house, followed by a stick person/people to represent them. Say the following three times:

I CALL UPON THE HORNED GOD FOR HELP IN BANISHING THESE PEOPLE FROM MY LIFE.

MAY THEY STOP CAUSING SO MUCH STRIFE. FROM DAY ONE, THE SPELL HAS BEGUN.

I CALL UPON YOUR POWER TO BRING ME PEACE ONCE AGAIN.

SO MOTE IT BE.

The important thing to remember is to really imagine how it would feel for these people to be removed from your life once and for all. You should have a feeling of hope and excitement at the prospect of the spell beginning to work. Blow out the candles one by one, starting with the orange one, then the black ones in an anticlockwise direction.

At the same time on day two, relight the candles in the same way as you did yesterday. Again, look into the flames while you contemplate the trouble your neighbours have caused. In the second section of your paper, draw a picture of your neighbours packing up boxes, getting ready to move out. Say the following three times:

I CALL UPON THE HORNED GOD TO WAVE THESE PEOPLE OFF FROM MY LIFE.

FROM DAY TWO, THE SPELL HAS BREWED. SO MOTE IT BE.

Blow out the candles again as per the day before as you visualize your joy at seeing the back of these nuisances.

On the third day, relight the candles in the same way. This time, focus your mind on your neighbours being gone from their property and a lovely new bunch of neighbours moving their stuff in. Draw a picture in the third section of the paper that represents this happening. Say the following three times:

I CALL UPON THE HORNED GOD. GOODBYE OLD AND HELLO NEW. MAY WE ALL LIVE IN PEACE.

SO MOTE IT BE.

Again, really imagine how you will feel when your old neighbours have left the property, and your nice new neighbours move in. Imagine saying hello to them and introducing yourself. Visualize them being the best neighbours you've ever had living next door to you.

This time, allow all the candles to burn down safely. Once the orange candle has almost burned down, light your piece of paper from its flame and carefully drop it into the fireproof dish or cauldron. Wait until all the paper has turned to ash.

Clear away all your spent candles and pour the paper ash into your envelope. This needs to be buried somewhere along the boundary between you and your neighbour. If you live in an apartment, bury it close by in a flower bed or flowerpot. You should now take your tourmaline crystal and put it somewhere safe outside of your home, where it will continue to protect you.

Be aware that this spell takes a while to kick in, because people don't just move house quickly. If nothing has happened by the next waning moon, repeat the spell.

'Clean Up Your Mess' Spell

PURPOSE

To make a housemate clear up after themselves

WHEN TO CAST

Any day and time during a new-moon phase

WHAT YOU NEED

an empty spray bottle

5 drops each of rosemary, lavender and peppermint essential oils

500ml tap water

a bunch of rosemary

a bunch of flowers and a vase

The problem with living with other people is that we all have different standards. Some like their personal and shared spaces to be neat and tidy; others are more laid back, and it doesn't matter to them if their home environment is messy or unclean. If you're sharing your home with other people and the mess is getting to you, try this clean-up spell.

WHAT TO DO

Thoroughly clean the messy areas of your home – no, it doesn't seem fair that you have to do the cleaning, but in order for this spell to work, you need be the bigger person and lead by example.

Add the essential oils to the spray bottle, along with the tap water. Shake the solution to mix. Go into every room and squirt your potion three times into the air. As you do so, sing the following:

**THE MESS HAS GONE, THE MESS HAS GONE
NOW WE CAN ALL MOVE ON.**

**THE MESS HAS CLEARED, THE MESS HAS
CLEARED
IT NO LONGER FALLS ON DEAF EARS.**

SO MOTE IT BE.

Place a sprig of rosemary in every room, including the bathroom, and pop one under your doormat. Arrange your flowers in the vase and add a couple of sprigs of rosemary to the display.

Fellow residents will begin to clear up their mess in future.

Spell To Find
A Lost Pet

PURPOSE

To find your beloved companion

WHEN TO CAST

Any day and time during any moon phase

WHAT YOU NEED

an item of your clothing

a yellow candle

a yellow Post-it note

a drawing pin

We all love our pets dearly, and if they go missing it is deeply worrying. I was given this spell when one of my dogs went missing in the woods, and within three days he was found again. Cast this spell the moment you realize your pet is missing.

WHAT TO DO

The first thing to do when your pet has gone missing is to place an item of your clothing, such as a scarf or a jumper, in the last place you saw them. Your scent will be on the item of clothing and will still be strong enough for your pet to find.

Next, light the yellow candle and focus your attention on your pet and their safety. Visualize them being OK where they are and sniffing the air to get back on track and find you again.

Write the name of your pet on to the yellow Post-it note and pin it to a wall that you will see every day. Say the following words:

[Name of pet], it's time to come home now.

You are safe and fit and healthy.

By the power of Luna,

I call you back to your home.
So mote it be.

Allow the candle to burn down safely.

Your four-legged best friend should return to the spot where you left your item of clothing very soon.

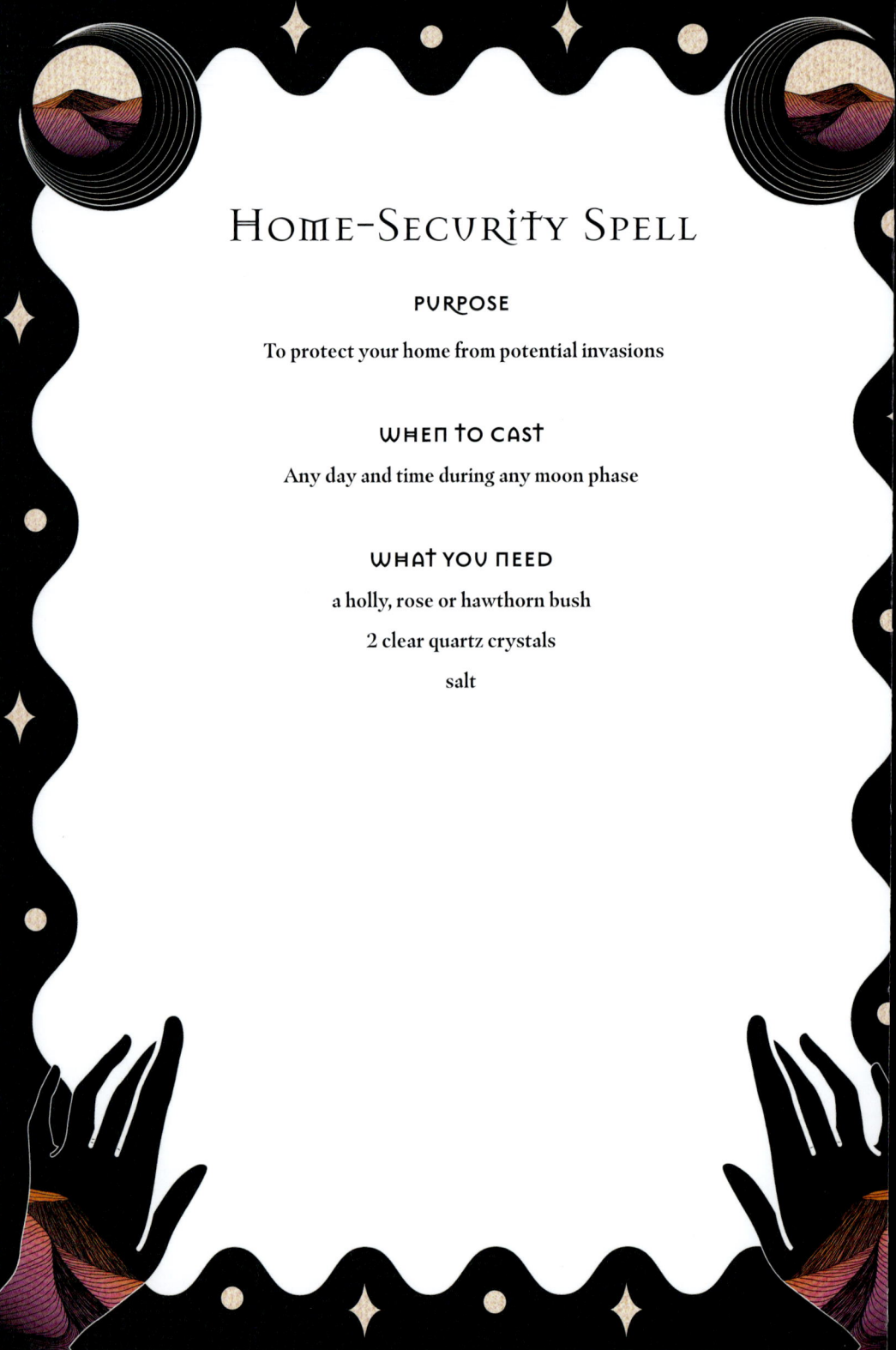

Home-Security Spell

PURPOSE

To protect your home from potential invasions

WHEN TO CAST

Any day and time during any moon phase

WHAT YOU NEED

a holly, rose or hawthorn bush

2 clear quartz crystals

salt

It's important to feel safe in your own home; it's a space where you should feel secure and protected. While gadgets such as home cameras and alarms are perfect to protect your home from intruders, it's always worth adding a little magic.

WHAT TO DO

The first thing to do is to purchase a holly, rose or hawthorn bush and place it outside your front door. If you live in an apartment or somewhere where you can't place a potted plant outside, find some holly leaves and place these on all the windowsills in your home.

Next, place one clear quartz crystal as close to your front door as possible, and the second close to the back door of your property (if you only have one door, just place them both there).

Finally, walk around the perimeter of your home, sprinkling a continuous line of salt. Again, if you live in an apartment or a property where it might be difficult to walk around the whole perimeter, draw a line of salt across the front and back thresholds.

Visualize an arc of protective white light completely covering your home. Do this several times during the day to build up the protective energy.

Your home will now be protected. You can also use the 'arc of white light' method to protect your car whenever it's parked up somewhere.

Repeat this spell every time you feel anxious about your home being invaded.

Threshold Protection Spell

PURPOSE

To protect your space from negative energy

WHEN TO CAST

Any time on a Wednesday, during any moon phase

WHAT YOU NEED

a small pouch

a pinch of salt

a pinch of dried lavender flowers

a pinch of dried red clover flowers

a pinch of dried nettle leaves

a key (preferably a copy of your house key or an old key)

a bowl

hot water

a clean cloth or sponge

a black permanent marker

You should feel safe in your own home, but sometimes negative energy from other people can infiltrate your space, making you feel uneasy instead of safe and secure. This threshold spell will help you take back your space and feel happy and secure there.

WHAT TO DO

Gather your ingredients together and focus your mind on making your home feel secure. Imagine that there is an invisible fortress around your home. As you do this, fill your pouch with the salt, lavender flowers, red clover flowers and dried nettle leaves. Now add the key to the pouch and tie it closed.

Next, fill a bowl with hot water and add the pouch you've created to the water. Leave it to steep for five minutes. Now take your cloth or sponge and draw this Nordic Bind Protection rune on to it with your marker pen. Allow the ink to dry.

Go around your home and wash all the surfaces, windows and doors with the water in the bowl and your rune cloth. Finally, wash your front and back doors. Allow to dry naturally.

Your home is now protected by magic, and you can feel safe once again. Repeat if you ever feel vulnerable in your own home.

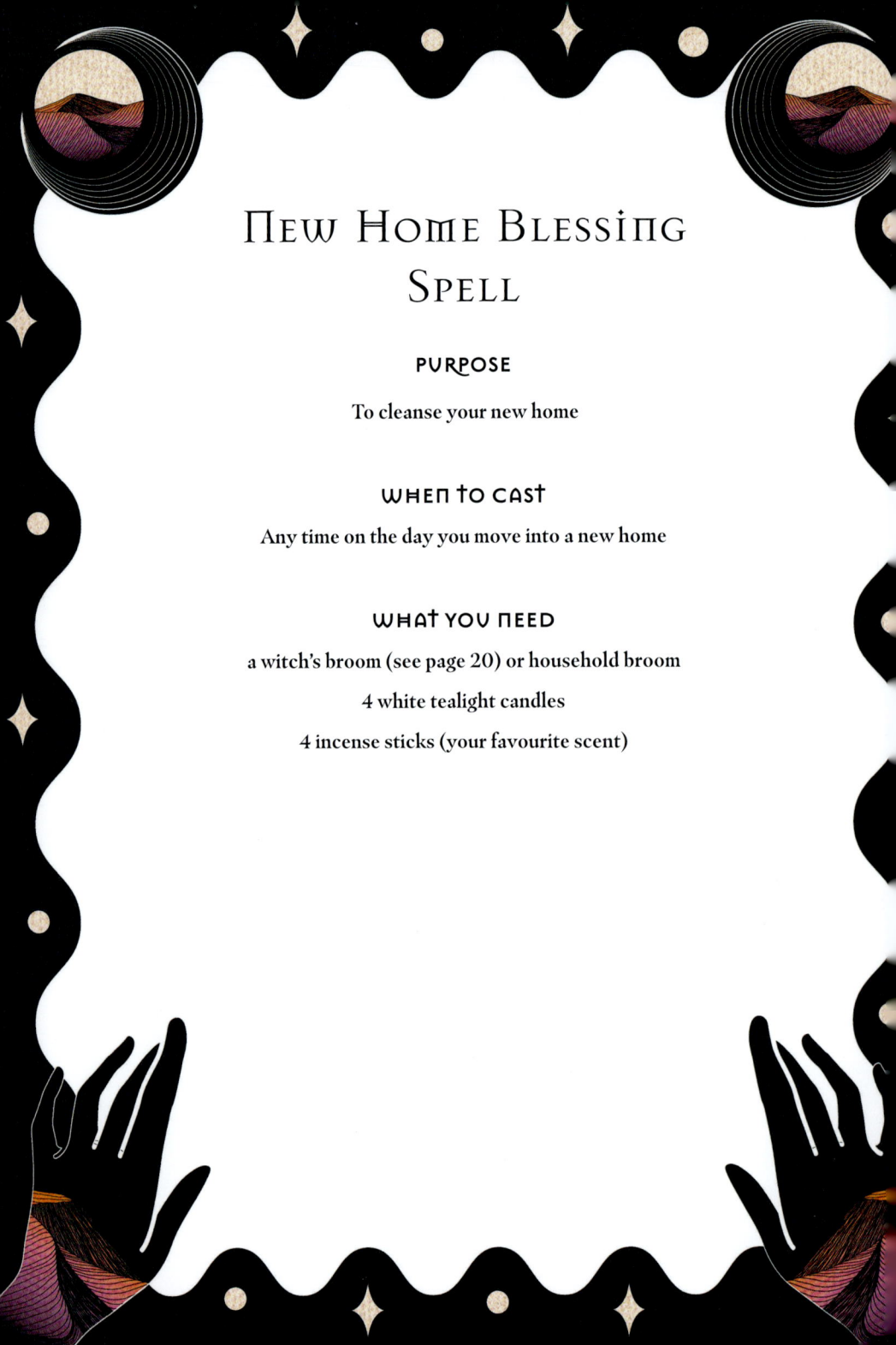

New Home Blessing Spell

PURPOSE

To cleanse your new home

WHEN TO CAST

Any time on the day you move into a new home

WHAT YOU NEED

a witch's broom (see page 20) or household broom

4 white tealight candles

4 incense sticks (your favourite scent)

When you move to a new home, it will always have residual energy left over from the previous occupants. Sometimes this is positive, other times it can be negative. Either way, it's better if you rid your home of any former occupants' energy so that you can start afresh.

WHAT TO DO

Stick an incense stick into each tealight candle, then place one in each corner of your new home (downstairs if it's a multi-floor property). Open the front door and sweep through every room as if you are sweeping any negative energy out of the front door.

Light all four candles and incense sticks, then say the following prayer:

I BLESS THE ROOF, I BLESS THE WALLS,
NOTHING BUT BLESSINGS HERE BEFALL.

I BLESS THIS HOME, AND ALL WITHIN,
NOTHING BUT GOOD CAN COME IN.

I BLESS MY HOME, I BLESS MY FAMILY,
TOGETHER WE WILL ALL LIVE HAPPILY.

THE FOUR QUARTERS ARE NOW PROTECTED,
AND ANY BAD ENERGY WILL BE REJECTED.

Allow the candles and incense to burn away. Turn your broom upside down and leave it by your front door for seven days. Your new home is now protected, and any negative energy has been dispelled.

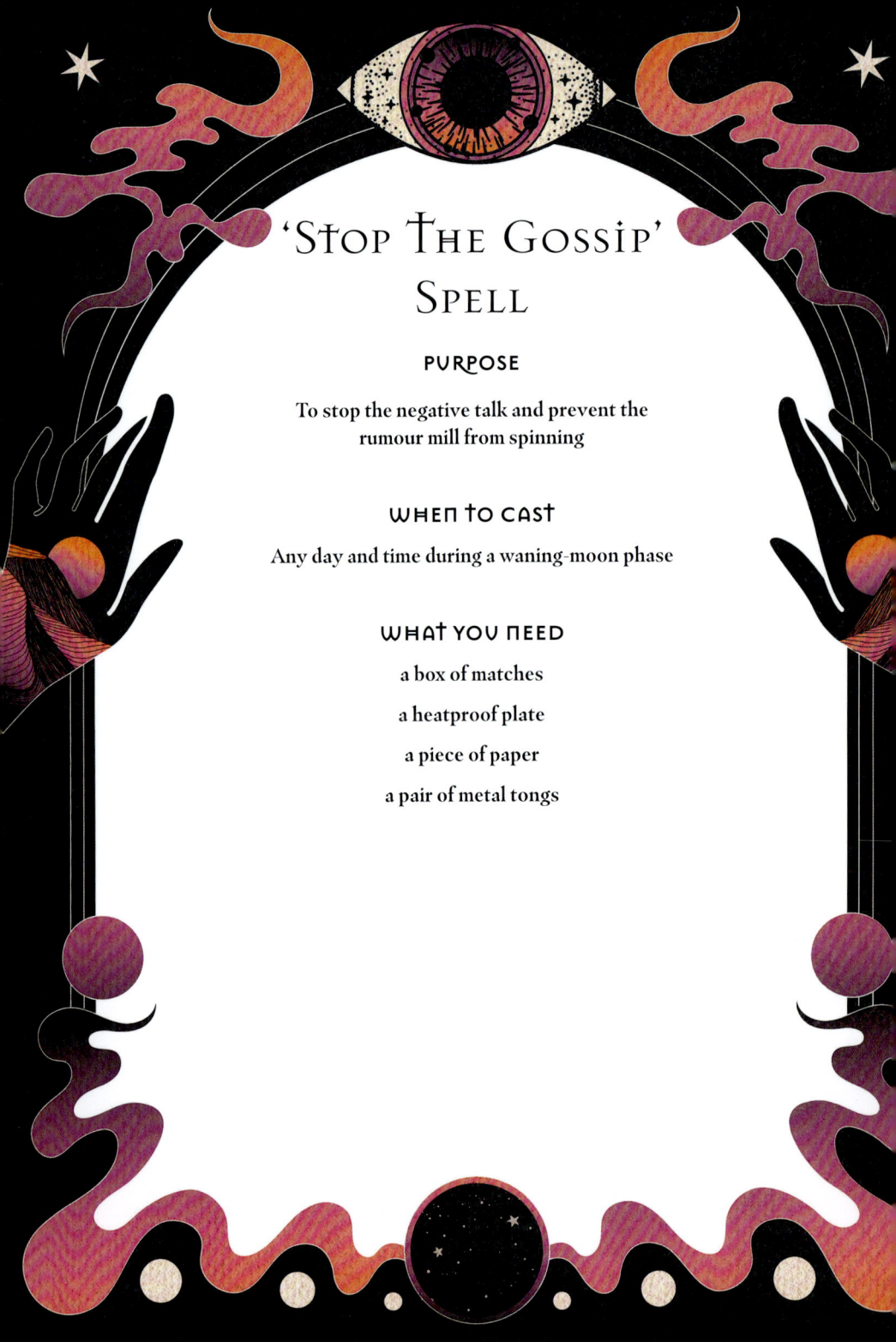

'Stop The Gossip' Spell

PURPOSE

To stop the negative talk and prevent the
rumour mill from spinning

WHEN TO CAST

Any day and time during a waning-moon phase

WHAT YOU NEED

a box of matches

a heatproof plate

a piece of paper

a pair of metal tongs

Everyone has been the subject of someone else's gossiping at some point – and likewise, I'm sure there are occasions where you've gossiped about someone else, because we are all prone to it from time to time. If you discover that you have people in your life who are nice to your face, but gossip about you behind your back, try this little spell to stop them in their tracks.

WHAT TO DO

Take nine matches out of the matchbox. Hold one over the plate and light it so that it burns all the way down – you will need to hold the unlit end of the matchstick with your metal tongs so that you don't burn yourself. Once it's completely burned down, you should be left with a long charcoal stick. Place it on the plate and repeat with the other eight matches so that you end up with nine charcoal sticks.

With the last burned match, write down the name or names of the person or people who have been gossiping about you on the piece of paper.

On top of the name(s), create a pentagram out of five of the spent matches (a five-sided star shape). Use the remaining matches to make a square around the pentacle. Say the following words:

GOSSIPS BE GONE
AND TAKE YOUR WORDS WITH YOU.

MAY YOU BE FOREVER SILENCED,
AND YOUR WORDS NOT BELIEVED
BY THOSE YOU CHOOSE TO GOSSIP TO.

MAY YOUR TONGUE BE QUIET
FROM HERE FORTH.

IT IS NOW SO.

Once the spell is complete, throw away the paper and matches. Anyone gossiping about you will now be silenced – and remember, by gossiping about you, they are affecting their own karma in a negative way.

Spell To Banish An Ex

PURPOSE

To get rid of an ex-partner for good

WHEN TO CAST

Any day and time during a waning- or new-moon phase

WHAT YOU NEED

salt

a piece of paper

a red pen

scissors

a jar with a lid

vinegar

tap water or spring water

a black tealight candle

1 bay leaf

A break-up is never easy, but it's harder for some to move on than others. Some people don't take rejection well and, with a bruised ego, they will do anything to get you back. If you have an ex who is still trying to get back with you, this witch's bottle banishing spell will keep them away with no harm done to them. A witch's bottle is an ancient spell that witches still use today, and you'll often find these bottles in the gardens of old houses.

WHAT TO DO

The first thing to do is to protect where you live by drawing a line of salt across the threshold of your home.

Next, draw a paper-doll figure on the piece of paper with the red pen. This will represent your ex, so make it as realistic as possible. Cut out the figure with the scissors, fold it in three and place it in the jar.

Pour salt into the jar until the paper figure is completely buried and you can no longer see it. Next add 13 drops of vinegar. Fill the rest of the jar with water, then seal the lid on securely and shake the jar vigorously while visualizing your ex just disappearing from your life. Say the following words:

I CALL UPON GODDESS BRIDGID TO PROTECT ME FROM [Name].

MAY YOU NOW BE ON YOUR WAY AND NEVER BOTHER ME AGAIN.

YOU ARE NOW BANISHED FAR, FAR AWAY.

SO MOTE IT BE.

While the contents of the jar settle, light the black candle, and put it on top of the jar lid. Allow it to safely burn down. Meanwhile, take the bay leaf and write your ex's name on the leaf in red pen. Place the bay leaf in a shoe that you regularly wear. Every time you walk, imagine you are stamping down the thought of your ex.

Once the black candle has burned down, take your jar outside and bury it in your garden. If you don't have a garden, you can simply throw it in a rubbish bin.

Your ex should slowly drift away now and no longer bother you.

Family Feud Spell

PURPOSE

To resolve family disputes

WHEN TO CAST

Any day and time during a new-moon phase

WHAT YOU NEED

a family photo, or a photo of the member you are feuding with
(if you don't have a photo, write their name or names on a
piece of paper instead)

a white tealight candle

a length of red cord

9 flower heads (choose your favourite type of flower)

They say you can't choose your family, and sometimes things can get tough when so many personalities are bonded by family ties. As you grow older, the people in your family grow older too, and might develop traits and nuances that you don't agree with. This can lead to arguments, fights or the feeling that you no longer really know a family member. If you want to get back on track with your family, try this spell to mend family feuds.

WHAT TO DO

Place the photo and candle in front of you. Light the candle and take the red cord in your hands. As you reflect on the issues you've had with your family or family member, look into the flame of the candle, and begin tying a knot in the red cord. If you are having issues with more than one family member, tie a knot for each of them, leaving a gap between each knot. Repeat the following words once for each family member.

AS ABOVE, SO BELOW,
MAKE AMENDS AND MAKE IT SO.

BRING HARMONY BACK INTO THE FOLD,
THE LOVE RETURNS TO HAVE AND TO HOLD.

THIS IS MY WISH.

Place the knotted cord on top of your photo, then take the nine flower heads and place them in a circle around the photo and candle.

Leave everything in its place until the candle has safely burned down. Keep the photo, cord and flower heads in a safe place for at least 28 days. You should soon see an improvement within your family dynamics.

Spell To Eliminate A Frenemy

PURPOSE

To get rid of a friend who never was

WHEN TO CAST

Any day and time during a waning-moon phase

WHAT YOU NEED

3 black tealight candles

a saucepan

water

a heatproof bowl

a pinch of earth from your garden or a plant pot

a pinch of salt and pepper

a cocktail stick

Sad as it may be, sometimes your best friends can become your worst enemies. Sometimes you just outgrow each other, and other times you simply can't forgive your friend for something they've done. However, harbouring resentment against someone who you thought was your ride-or-die doesn't do you any good, so the best thing to do is to eliminate them from your life. This spell, originally from the spiritual tradition of Hoodoo folk magic, will help you to let go and move on from someone who was once your bestie. Whenever people hear the word 'Hoodoo', they automatically think it's associated with black magic. It isn't; Hoodoo is the name given to African American folk magic, and no one will get hurt by this spell.

WHAT TO DO

Place the three black tealight candles in a triangle shape and light them all. Half-fill the saucepan with water and place on the stove over a low heat. Place the heatproof bowl over the top. As the candles burn down, carefully tip any liquid wax into the bowl. The heat from the water will keep the wax soft. Keep doing this as your candles burn down.

Add the earth, salt and pepper to the warm candle wax in the bowl and mix it all together with the cocktail stick. Once all the ingredients are mixed into the wax, carefully take the dish off the saucepan, and allow the wax mixture to cool a little so that it can be easily moulded. Take the wax mixture in your hands and roll it into a little ball. When you have created a ball, flatten it between the palms of your hands and make a flat human shape out of the wax (head, body, arms and legs).

As you do this, recite the words below:

[NAME OF PERSON YOU WISH TO LEAVE],
UP, UP AND AWAY YOU GO.

NOW YOU'RE JUST SOMEONE THAT I USED TO KNOW.

I PROTECT MY SPIRIT AND I PROTECT MY SOUL,
YOUR POISON IS NOW TRAPPED WITHIN THIS DOLL.

IT IS NOW SO.

Allow the wax figure to go hard. To finish the spell, snap the head off the shoulders of the wax figure and throw both parts into the bin. Your frenemy will no longer be able to contact you.

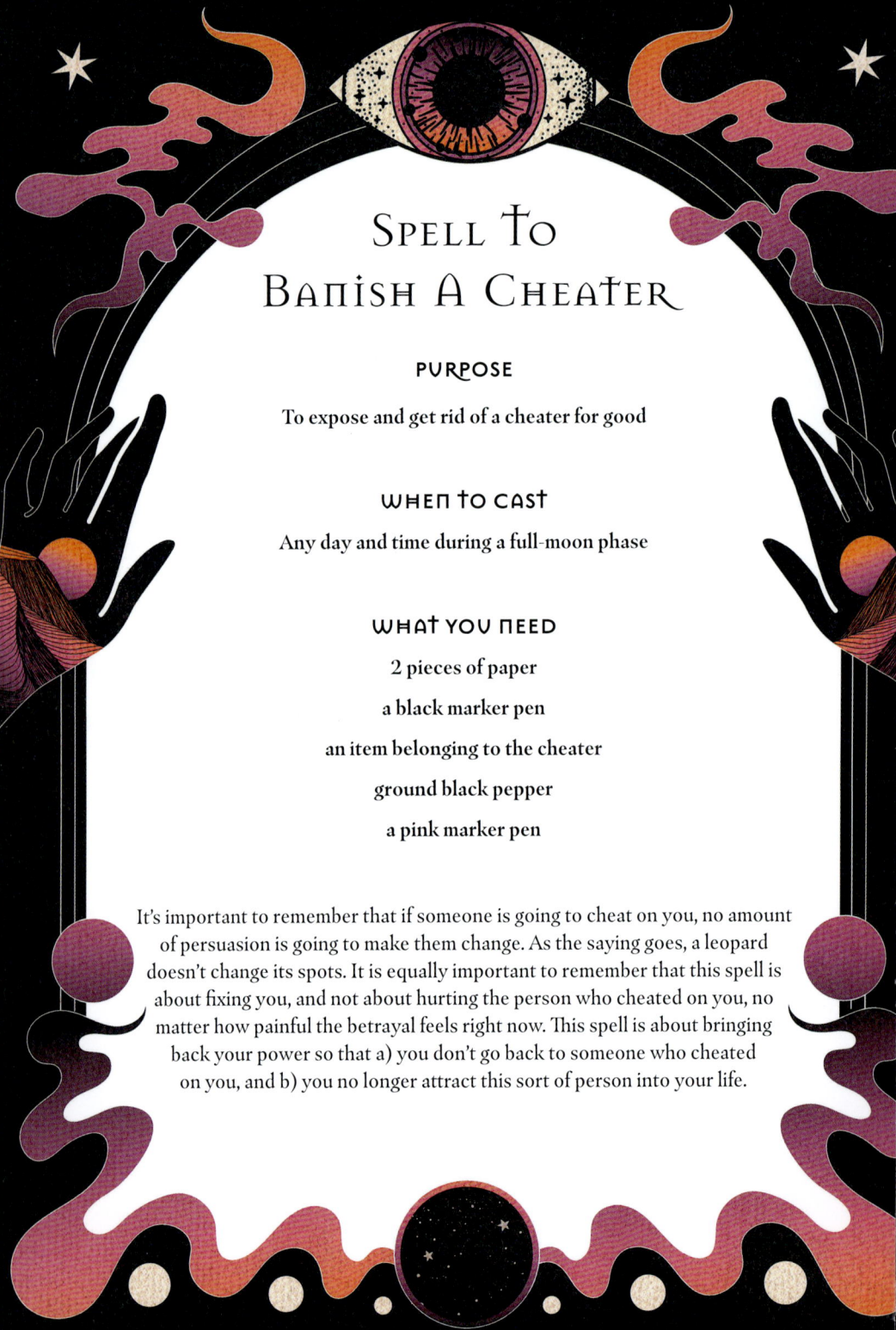

Spell To Banish A Cheater

PURPOSE

To expose and get rid of a cheater for good

WHEN TO CAST

Any day and time during a full-moon phase

WHAT YOU NEED

2 pieces of paper

a black marker pen

an item belonging to the cheater

ground black pepper

a pink marker pen

It's important to remember that if someone is going to cheat on you, no amount of persuasion is going to make them change. As the saying goes, a leopard doesn't change its spots. It is equally important to remember that this spell is about fixing you, and not about hurting the person who cheated on you, no matter how painful the betrayal feels right now. This spell is about bringing back your power so that a) you don't go back to someone who cheated on you, and b) you no longer attract this sort of person into your life.

WHAT TO DO

Find some time when you can be alone for an hour or so. In the centre of the first piece of paper, draw a large pentagram with the black marker pen. Place the item belonging to the cheater in the centre of the pentagram. This could be a hair belonging to the person or a personal possession such as a toothbrush. If you don't have anything belonging to them, write their full name and date of birth in the centre of the pentagram.

In each of the five-star points, put a black cross mark, and around the outside of the pentagram write any words that you feel about this person right now – anger, hurt, disappointment, pain, sadness etc. Allow yourself time to feel your emotions about this person. If you need to cry or shout, do so.

Sprinkle the black pepper over the piece of paper and say the following words:

[NAME], I BANISH YOU FROM MY WORLD
AS I NOW TRY TO REBUILD.

YOUR ACTIONS HAVE BETRAYED ME THIS DAY

SO I NOW SEND YOU ON YOUR WAY.

NO LONGER WILL I LET YOU IN,
AND NOW MY LIFE WITHOUT YOU BEGINS.

When you're done, rip up the paper and dispose of it and the personal item in the bin. Next, take the second piece of paper and draw another large pentagram in the centre, this time with the pink marker pen.

In each of the five-star points, draw a love heart, then around the rest of the page, write down positive words about yourself – kind, caring, loving, fun, etc. If you have trouble doing this, ask a friend to tell you how amazing you are.

Remind yourself that this has nothing to do with you as a person, because if the cheater is willing to cheat on you, they will do the same with anyone. Say the following words out loud:

I CALL UPON THE GODDESS FREYA TO HELP ME
FIND MY WAY BACK

TO SELF-WORTHINESS, LOVE AND
EMPOWERMENT.

FROM TODAY I TAKE BACK MY POWER,

AND NO LONGER ATTRACT LESS THAN MY
WORTH.

SO IT WILL BE.

Keep this piece of paper with you in your purse or wallet, and anytime you feel down about the cheater, take out the paper and read it to remind yourself of what an amazing person you are.

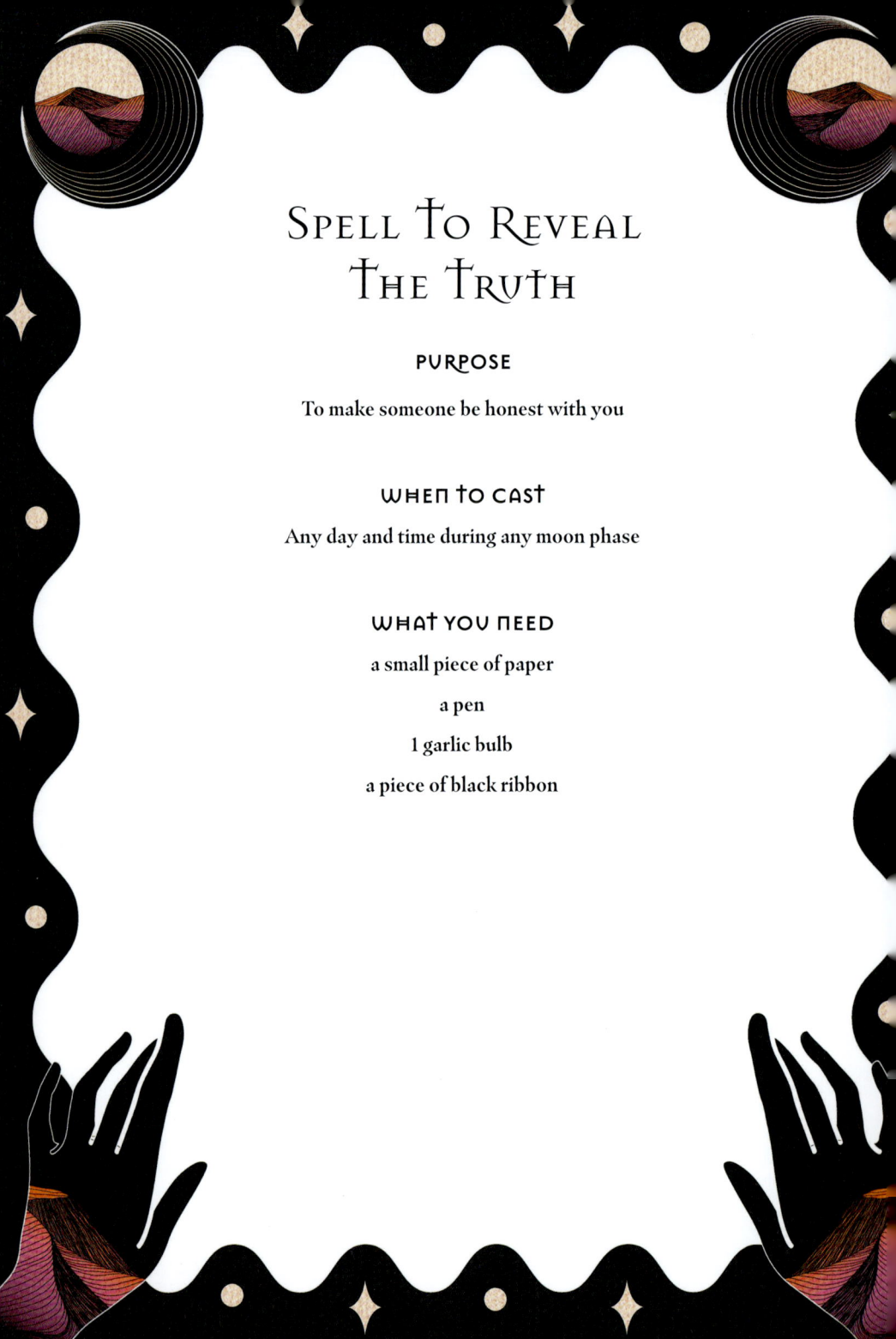

Spell To Reveal The Truth

PURPOSE

To make someone be honest with you

WHEN TO CAST

Any day and time during any moon phase

WHAT YOU NEED

a small piece of paper

a pen

1 garlic bulb

a piece of black ribbon

Sometimes you just know that someone is lying to you, and yet no one else believes you. This spell will bring the truth to light and prove that your intuition was right.

WHAT TO DO

Take the piece of paper and write down the name or names of whoever has been lying to you. Underneath the name(s), draw a set of scales, like those on the Justice card in the Tarot. Next, cut the garlic bulb in half vertically and fold up the piece of paper so that it's small enough to be placed in between the two halves.

Close the two halves of the garlic bulb together, then wind the black ribbon around it to hold it closed. Tie the ribbon with three knots to secure it.

Hold the garlic bulb in both hands and visualize the truth coming out. Keep the bulb in your fridge or freezer for three nights, and then bury it somewhere away from your home. The liar or liars will soon be exposed.

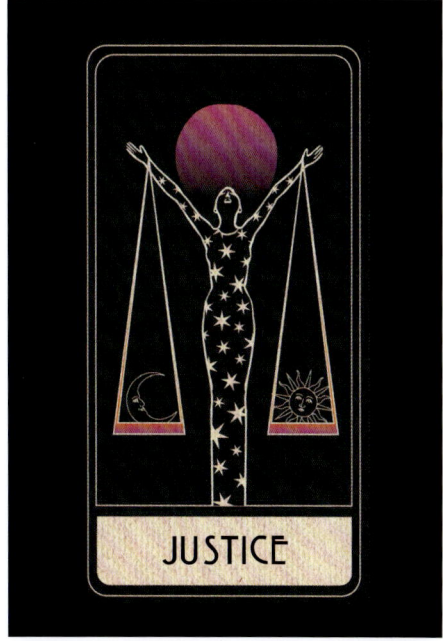

JUSTICE

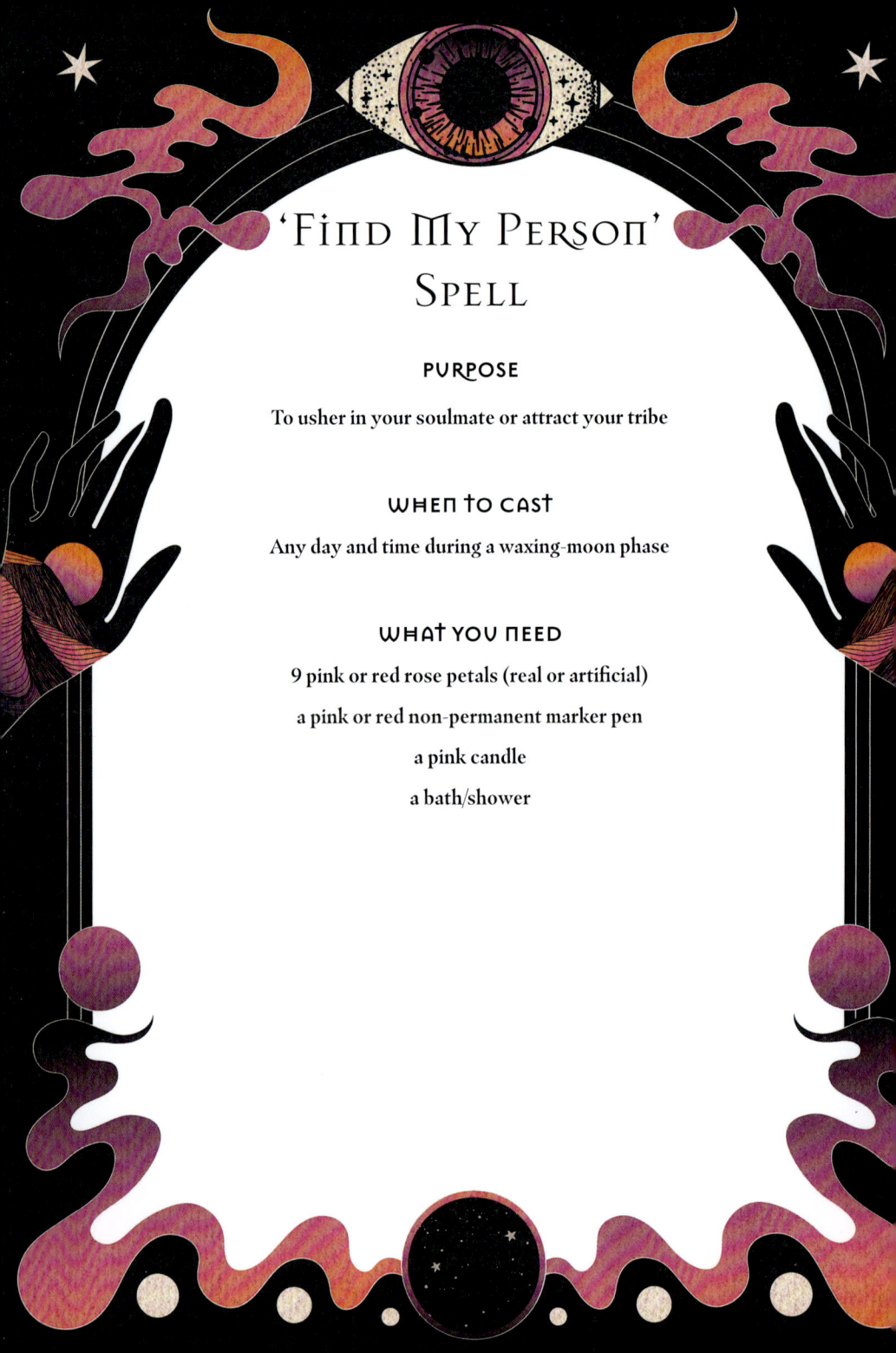

'Find My Person' Spell

PURPOSE

To usher in your soulmate or attract your tribe

WHEN TO CAST

Any day and time during a waxing-moon phase

WHAT YOU NEED

9 pink or red rose petals (real or artificial)

a pink or red non-permanent marker pen

a pink candle

a bath/shower

Have you ever wanted so badly to find 'your person', only to make the mistake of putting all your focus on someone who is simply not the best fit? Think of it like going to a shoe shop: some shoes look ideal but they don't fit you, or they are out of stock, or they just don't look as good on as they did in the window. This spell will help you to find the person (or people) truly meant for you.

WHAT TO DO

Take a rose petal and write on it something to represent what your ideal person is like, for example: 'kind', 'caring', 'passionate', 'brown eyes', 'six feet tall'. Repeat with all nine rose petals, writing a different quality on each one.

Light your candle and arrange the petals around it. Allow the candle to safely burn down as you visualize your ideal person coming into your life. It's important to remember that you don't have to worry about how you will meet this person. Just surrender it to the universe.

Once the candle has burned down, collect all the rose petals, run yourself a bath or shower and scatter the petals either in the bath water or in the shower tray. Imagine the universe picking out the perfect person for you, who will be exactly as you've specified.

After you've finished, you can discard the rose petals and wait while the universe finds your perfect person.

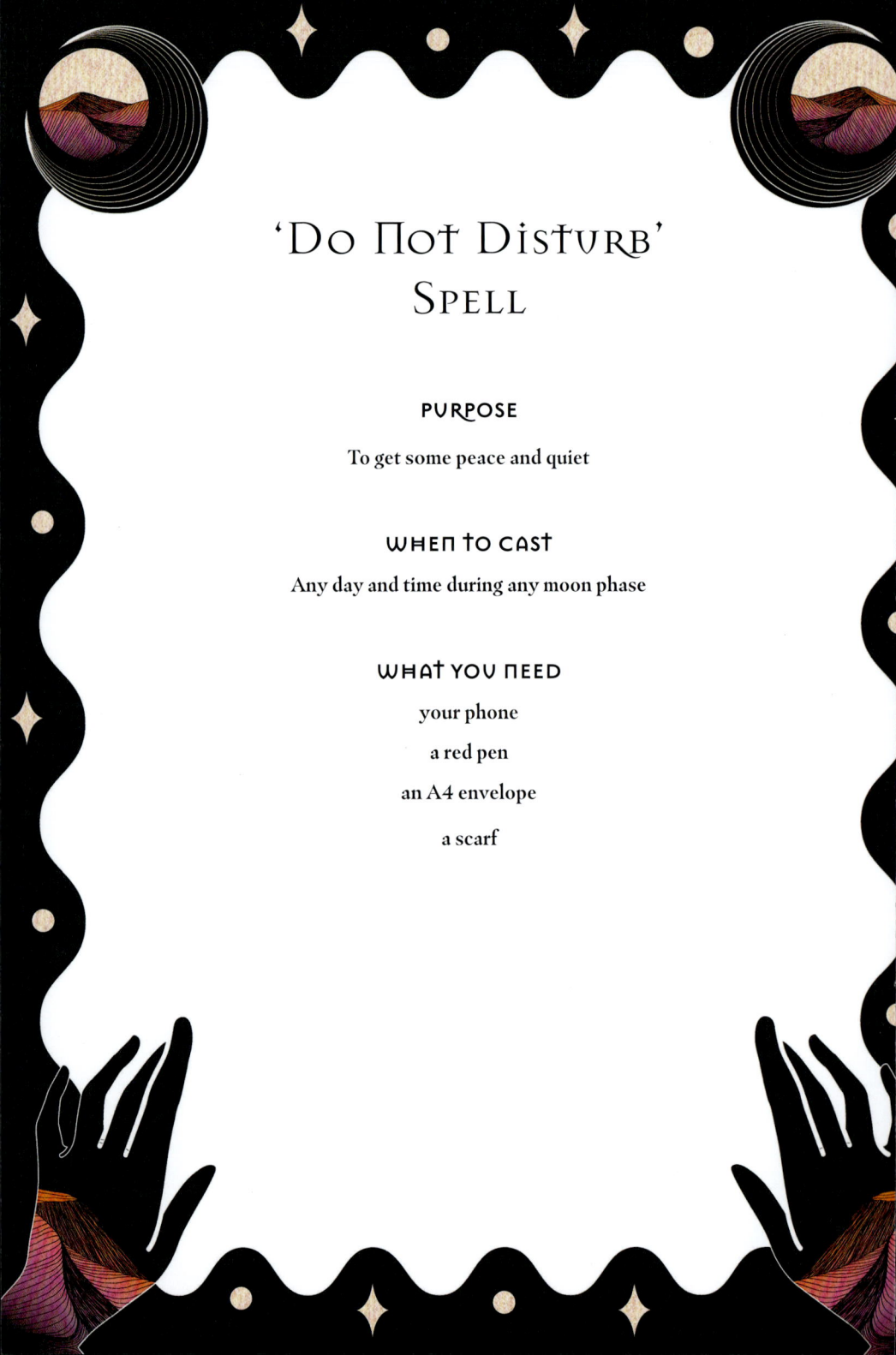

'Do Not Disturb' Spell

PURPOSE

To get some peace and quiet

WHEN TO CAST

Any day and time during any moon phase

WHAT YOU NEED

your phone

a red pen

an A4 envelope

a scarf

You know what it's like: from the minute you wake up to the time you go to bed, your phone pings with notifications. Given that people have access to us 24 hours a day now, it's little wonder that we feel anxious and yet unable to just turn off our devices – but trust me when I say it's perfectly OK to be uncontactable for a while. Sometimes you just want to switch off from the world and tell everyone to leave you alone. Yes, we can simply turn off notifications, but as soon as you turn them back on, they will be there, waiting for you. This spell will stop people thinking about contacting you until you are ready to hear from them. And if there is something really important, people will get hold of you another way.

WHAT TO DO

First thing to do is to turn off your phone completely – not just your notifications. Next, take your red pen and large envelope and draw a big circle in the centre of the envelope, then a cross inside the circle. Put your phone into the envelope and seal it. Imagine the universe sending the message 'Do Not Disturb Me' to all the contacts in your phone and on social media/messenger. Wrap the envelope in the scarf. This ensures that no negative energy can escape to you. Leave the wrapped envelope in another room for at least an hour. As you leave the room, shake your arms and hands as if you are letting go of technology for a while, then go and do something you've been meaning to do, such as cleaning out a drawer or reading a chapter of a book.

After a minimum of one hour (it can be longer if you feel happy to leave it longer), you can take your phone back out of the envelope. Recycle the envelope and turn your phone back on. You should find that people will now respect your privacy and will only contact you about urgent matters.

Repeat this spell every time you need a technology break.

'Calm the Storm' Spell

PURPOSE

To help quieten your mind and cast away anxious thoughts

WHEN TO CAST

Any day and time during any moon phase

WHAT YOU NEED

a white candle

a pestle and mortar (or bowl and spoon)

1 teaspoon dried basil

1 teaspoon dried oregano

1 teaspoon dried mint

1 teaspoon dried sage

1 teaspoon lavender flowers

1 teaspoon cornflour

a small charm bag

a small rose quartz crystal

Anxiety can be debilitating, especially when you can't see any light at the end of the tunnel. You wouldn't think it, but anxiety is actually your brain trying to keep you safe, and it's often a good thing. However, sometimes it can end up convincing you that you are in danger all the time, which prevents you from functioning as you should. In a world of social-media 'likes', oversharing and over-caring, it's little wonder that you might become overwhelmed. As with any other medical condition, this is not a fix-all, and I advise you to seek medical advice if your suffering is inhibiting your daily life. But know that you are not alone and that you are very much perfect as you are. This spell will help you to feel reassured if the world becomes too overwhelming for you. The important thing to remember during this spell is that you are safe, and that this is just a temporary thought in your head. It's not a real threat to your life.

WHAT TO DO

Light your candle and imagine that the light from the flame is where you can feel safe and protected. Take a few deep breaths and mix the herbs, lavender and cornflour into your mortar or bowl, then use the pestle or the back of a spoon to grind them all together as you repeat the following words three times:

THIS IS TEMPORARY AND I AM SAFE.

THIS IS MY SPACE
TO FEEL SAFE ON THIS BLESSED DAY.

IT'S ALL OK, I AM OK.

Try to grind the ingredients as finely as possible. Next, pour your ingredients into a small charm bag as you say the words for a fourth time, and add your rose quartz. Allow your candle to burn down safely.

You can now carry your protection bag with you. Whenever you feel anxious, take out this little charm bag and massage it in your hands, take three deep breaths and repeat the words again. Your anxiety will soon disappear.

'New Year, New Me' Spell

PURPOSE

To help you have a fabulous year

WHEN TO CAST

Any day and time during any moon phase

WHAT YOU NEED

a clean glass bottle/jar with a lid

tap water

3 teaspoons dried peppermint

3 teaspoons dried rosemary

3 teaspoons ground cinnamon

3 teaspoons ground ginger

1 teaspoon salt

a piece of paper

a gold pen

a candle

a wax stamp (optional)

Despite being called a New Year spell, this spell can in fact be cast anytime of the year. Every new day can be a fresh start if you want it to be. This spell encourages you to focus on what you want the next 12 months of your life to look like.

WHAT TO DO

Set aside some time for yourself when you know you will be undisturbed.

Fill your bottle or glass jar halfway with water. Next add the herbs, spices and salt, one at a time. A good way to do this if you are using a bottle is to make a small cone out of paper to function as a funnel. Place the lid back on to the bottle or jar and give it a good shake, then set this aside to rest.

Sit with your piece of paper and, using the gold pen, write down how you would like your life to be in 12 months' time. Who do you really want to be? What do you want to do for work? How much money do you want/need? With whom do you want to share your life? Write down all your wishes – and remember, you can be as extravagant as you like. No one is going to see this other than you.

When you're happy with your list, shake your bottle of 'New Me' potion again, then sprinkle a little on to the paper before replacing the lid. Allow the paper to dry, then fold it into three and seal with some warm wax. You can do this lighting a candle and dripping the melted wax on to the paper, then allowing it to cool, or you can use a special wax stamp designed to seal letters.

Keep your letter to yourself somewhere safe for the next 12 months. You can keep your 'New Me' potion for use whenever you want to make a wish come true. Just repeat the process.

Invisibility Cloak Spell

PURPOSE

To help you blend in when you are feeling self-conscious

WHEN TO CAST

Any day and time during a new-moon phase

WHAT YOU NEED

a white candle

sandalwood essential oil

How great would it be if you had an invisibility cloak? Well, it's not just for Harry Potter! Granted, you won't actually be invisible, but it will feel as though you are to the rest of the world. This can be useful if you have a big spot on your face that you don't want anyone to notice during your meeting, or maybe you are at a party and want to listen to some juicy information without everyone knowing you've entered the room. Despite there being only two ingredients in the spell, don't be fooled; it's very powerful! The power comes from the belief of your mind and your energy.

WHAT TO DO

Find a place where you can spend 15 minutes in peace and quiet. Anoint your candle with the sandalwood oil, then add a drop of oil to each wrist and one to your third-eye chakra – the centre of your forehead. Light your candle and watch the flame grow. As it does so, imagine being wrapped in a silver blanket (like the ones they use at the end of a marathon). This is your invisibility cloak. Keep visualizing this for 15 minutes.

When you feel as though you are fully wrapped up, blow out the candle. Now when you go out, you will be amazed at how people literally look right through you, and you can get on with your life without being recognized or noticed. This spell works every single time, and will last for as long as you wish it to.

If you wish to repeat the spell, anoint the candle and yourself again.

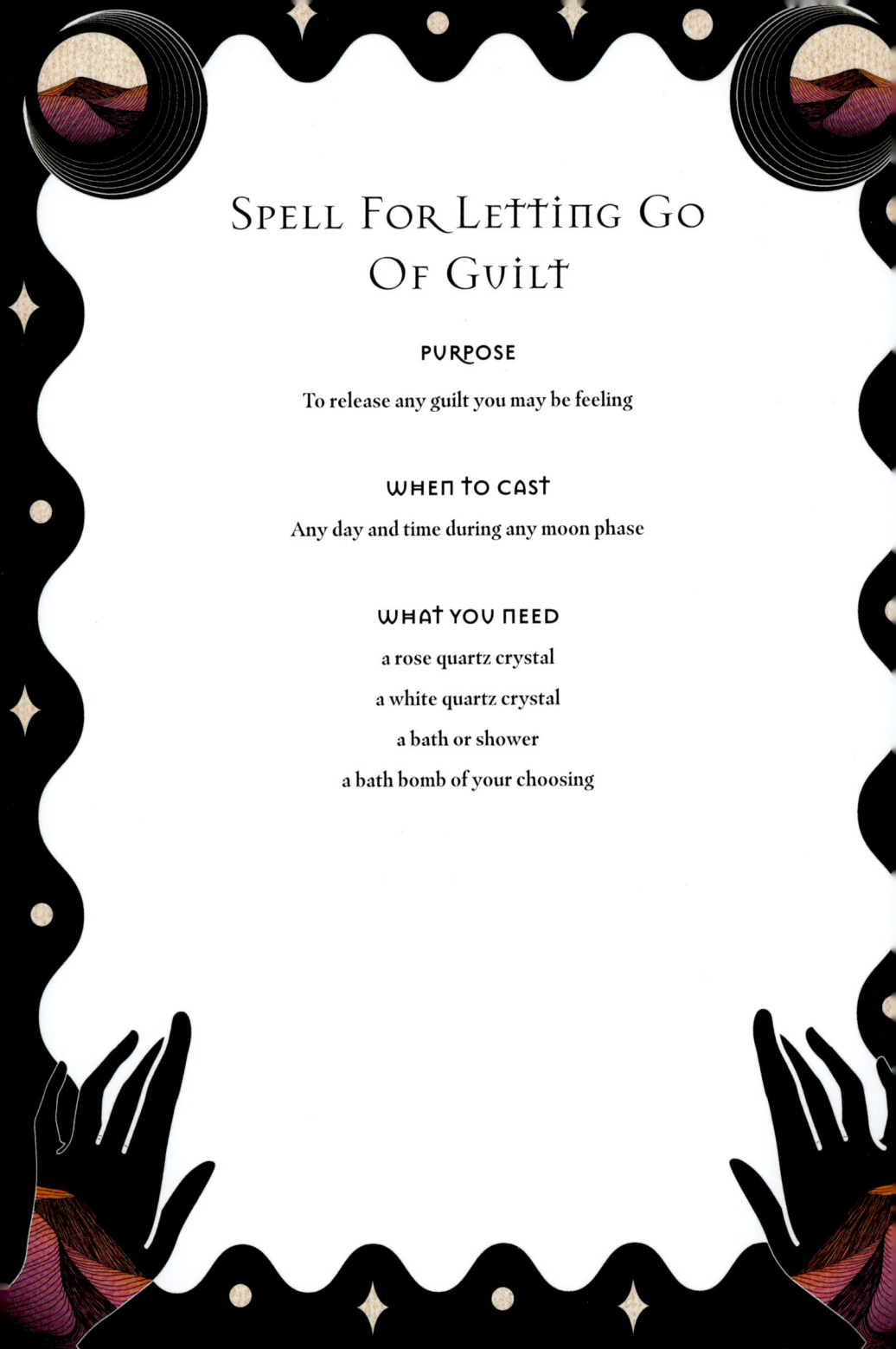

Spell For Letting Go Of Guilt

PURPOSE

To release any guilt you may be feeling

WHEN TO CAST

Any day and time during any moon phase

WHAT YOU NEED

a rose quartz crystal

a white quartz crystal

a bath or shower

a bath bomb of your choosing

We all have times when we feel guilty. Maybe you snapped at someone because you were tired. Maybe you asked to spend time on your own and are now worried you hurt a friend's feelings. Or perhaps you decided to end a relationship and hurt someone who loved you because it wasn't working. Whatever it might be, you do not need to feel guilt or remorse, as long as you haven't deliberately set out to hurt someone. This spell will help you to feel better and let go of any guilt you may be feeling.

WHAT TO DO

Gather up your ingredients and draw a bath or switch on your shower. If you're having a bath, drop the rose and white quartz crystals in first, followed by the bath bomb. If you're having a shower, place the crystals in the shower tray and hold the bath bomb in your hands. Step into the bath or shower and, as the bath bomb fizzles, imagine it magically absorbing any guilt you might be feeling, replacing it with clean and light energy. Say the following words as you wash yourself:

Guilt, guilt, set me free,
Guilt, guilt, hear my plea.

No longer do I feel guilty.

I am now free,
So mote it be.

Soak in the bath for 30 minutes, or stand under the shower for 5–10 minutes, visualizing your guilt going down the plug hole when you let the water out. By the time you have dried yourself off, you should have absolved any guilty feelings.

'Get My Mojo Back' Spell

PURPOSE

To help you feel like you again

WHEN TO CAST

Any day and time during any moon phase

WHAT YOU NEED

a yellow birthday candle

an orange birthday candle

1 small cupcake

a few sprigs of rosemary

Sometimes life can throw you a whole ball-pit of curveballs, and it feels as though you've been given a good old dose of bad karma despite being a good person. This feeling can deplete you, and you might find you've lost your happy-go-lucky self. This little spell will help you to get your mojo back.

WHAT TO DO

Place the two candles into your cupcake, then arrange the rosemary sprigs in a circle around the cake. As you do so, say the following words:

I CALL TO THE TRIPLE GODDESS
TO BRING BACK THE JOY IN MY LIFE.

MAY I NOW FEEL MYSELF AGAIN.
MY MOJO IS BACK FOR ALL TO SEE,

I AM AMAZING AND I LOVE ME!

Blow out the candles and visualize the happy colours of orange and yellow filling you up again – then eat the cake, because you deserve it!

Self-Care Spell

PURPOSE

To make yourself feel better

WHEN TO CAST

Any day and time during any moon phase

WHAT YOU NEED

your favourite happy music

a bath or shower

a yellow candle

a bunch of yellow flowers

a facemask

a glass of your favourite drink

We all have days, weeks or months when we feel in desperate need of a pick-me-up. You may have been going through a rough time with your partner, kids or friends, or you might be hating the job you're in right now. Regardless of what might be going on in your life, always remember that it will pass, and in six months' time you will have forgotten about what's going on right now and will be in a much better place. In the meantime, spoil yourself with this little pick-me-up spell.

WHAT TO DO

It's been proven that happy, feel-good music can have a super-positive effect on your mood, so to begin with choosing a track that makes you feel happy and like you want to dance. Play this song as you prepare your bath or shower. Light your yellow candle and sing along to your favourite tune as you get undressed.

Next, pluck the petals from your yellow flowers and throw them into either the bath or the shower tray. Keep six petals to one side. Prepare your facemask prior to getting into the shower or bath, and slather it all over your face. Now, before it dries, stick the six remaining petals to your face and look at yourself in the mirror. A smile will come across your face. Say the following:

CHEER ME UP, BUTTERCUP,
MAY THIS SADNESS PASS QUICKLY.

CHEER ME UP, BUTTERCUP,
MAY JOY COME BACK SWIFTLY.

CHEER ME UP, BUTTERCUP,
MAY THIS TEMPORARY FEELING BE GONE.

Jump into the bath or shower with your favourite drink and relax for a few minutes as you reflect on this feeling of sadness being just a temporary glitch.

When you're ready, wash off your facemask and watch the water flow away, along with your worries and sad feelings. Finish your drink, get dry, and you will feel 100 per cent better – I promise you.

Birthday Spell

PURPOSE

To ensure the year ahead is fabulous for you

WHEN TO CAST

Any time on your birthday

WHAT YOU NEED

3 pink candles to represent self-love

a birthday cake

sheets of edible rice paper

an icing pen in your favourite colour

Who doesn't love a birthday? Even if you're celebrating alone, you are still absolutely worthy of marking the day you graced the world with your presence. Do this little birthday spell anytime on your birthday.

WHAT TO DO

Find a time in the day when you have a spare five minutes. Place the three pink candles into your cake so that they form a triangle, which represents the power of the Triple Goddess (see page 39). Light the candles. Next, take a piece of edible rice paper, and with the icing pen, write a wish for the forthcoming year, then eat the paper. Repeat this two more times, writing the same wish each time.

Now say the following:

HAPPY BIRTHDAY TO ME,
HAPPY BIRTHDAY DEAR.

MAY MY WISHES COME TRUE
FOR THE FOLLOWING YEAR.

Close your eyes and blow out the candles, working in a clockwise direction. Your wishes will come true within 12 months – now go and eat that cake!

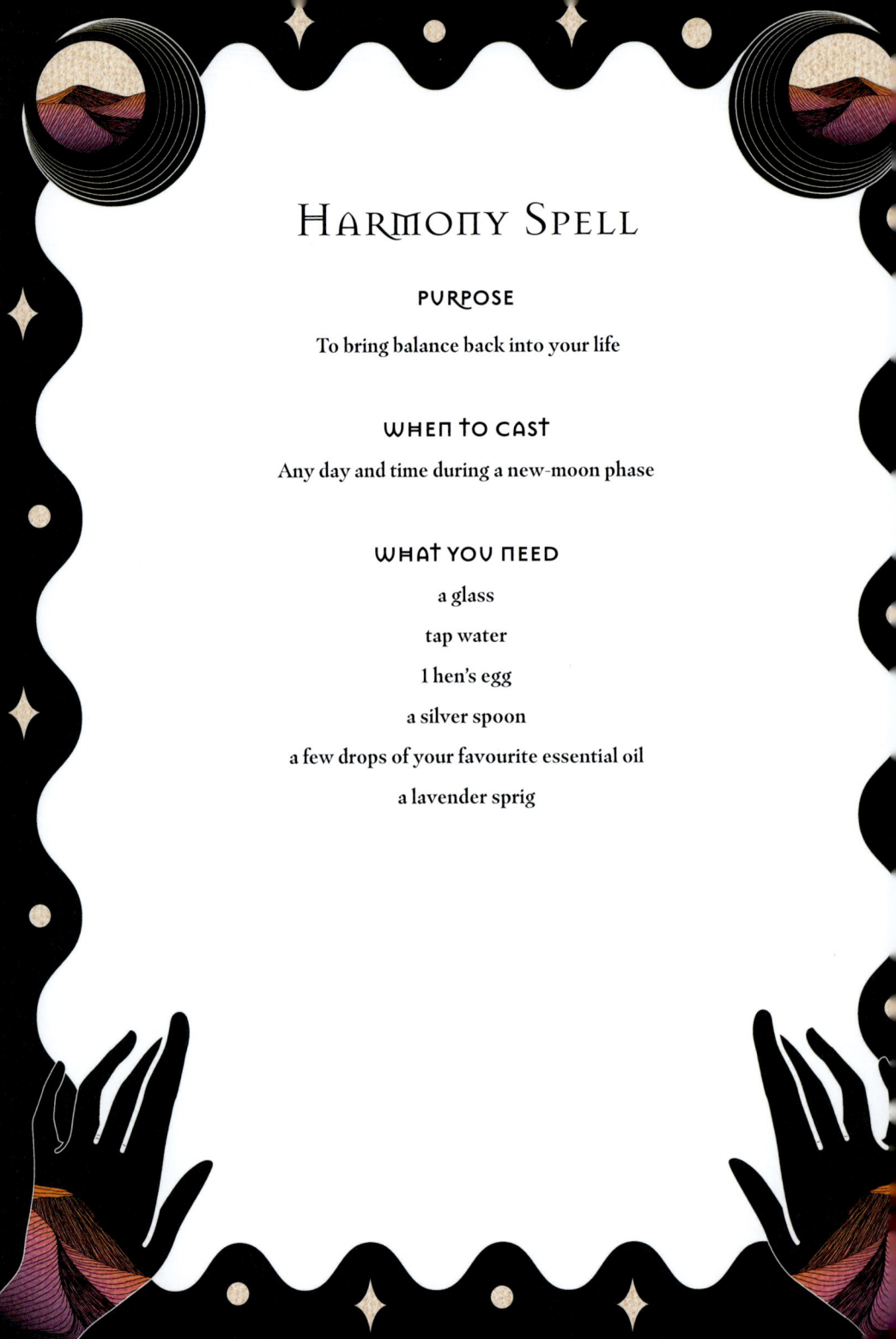

Harmony Spell

PURPOSE

To bring balance back into your life

WHEN TO CAST

Any day and time during a new-moon phase

WHAT YOU NEED

a glass

tap water

1 hen's egg

a silver spoon

a few drops of your favourite essential oil

a lavender sprig

We all have times in our lives when things simply don't go to plan – that's just how life is sometimes. However, you can make the rough times go away as quickly as they came by casting this little spell to quickly bring harmony back into your life.

WHAT TO DO

Fill your glass two-thirds of the way up with water, then carefully hold the egg in your dominant hand. Eggs are a sign of new beginnings and rebirth. You need to visualize new beginnings coming to you – and by holding the egg in your hand, your thoughts will penetrate the shell, to give birth to a harmonious new beginning for you.

When you feel ready, swish the water in a clockwise direction with the silver spoon to create a mini whirlpool, then break the egg into the water. It will spin in the glass. Add a few drops of your essential oil, followed by the lavender sprig. If you don't have fresh lavender, you can use dried instead. Stir the potion in the glass once more as you say the following words:

BY MY POWER, I SEND THIS TIME INTO A SPIN.

MAY THE PAST GO INTO THE BIN.

FROM HERE FORTH, I BRING IN HARMONY, AND NOTHING BAD CAN GET TO ME.

Allow the liquid to stop spinning on its own. When it has settled, take the glass outside and pour the solution outside the threshold of your home. If you live in an apartment or you don't have a threshold, simply take it outside somewhere near to your home and dispose of it there.

You will see harmony return to your life very soon.

'Say Goodbye To Anger' Spell

PURPOSE

To dispel anger and resentment

WHEN TO CAST

Any day and time during a new-moon phase

WHAT YOU NEED

a pink candle

a small piece of paper

a pink pen

a pink rose bush in a pot

a rose quartz crystal

It's not easy when you've been hurt by someone and you just can't seem to forgive and forget them. But, as the adage goes, holding on to anger is like drinking poison and expecting the other person to die. Obviously, I'm not encouraging anyone to wish death on another person, and this book is all about protecting your inner peace rather than seeking revenge upon another. To that end, this spell will help you to move on from the anger and the hurt and get on with your amazing life.

WHAT TO DO

Light your pink candle. On the piece of paper, write down the name of the person or people who have done you wrong, and then write down how sad it has made you feel. Write it as though you are writing a note to them. Get everything off your chest. When you feel satisfied, roll the paper into a tight scroll.

Take your potted rose bush and make a small hole in the soil, big enough for you to bury the scroll. As you push it into the soil, say:

I NOW RELEASE THE PAIN YOU CAUSED ME, AND I SEND YOU ON YOUR WAY.

Place a bit of soil over the hole you made and water your plant. Place your rose quartz crystal on top of the soil you disturbed, and leave the pot on a windowsill overnight. You will feel a lot lighter the following morning. You can either leave your plant on your windowsill or plant it in your garden. As it grows, you will find that you can move on; your anger will lessen, and you will accept that what has happened is now in the past.

Time-Out Spell

PURPOSE

To give yourself a break

WHEN TO CAST

Any day and time during any moon phase

WHAT YOU NEED

a purple candle

your phone, tablet or laptop (whatever you use most to keep in touch with others)

an amethyst crystal

We all need some time away from others, particularly when we are so accessible these days. With our phones and social media, we are effectively on call 24 hours a day, and it's near impossible for us to have some time to ourselves. This spell will magically put people on hold for as long as you wish, so that you can get back to just being your true self.

WHAT TO DO

To get some of your time back without appearing rude, light your purple candle and set the intention that as of now, you are unavailable. Take your phone, tablet or laptop, and find a notes app. Create a new note and write the following words: 'I am unavailable until [insert date].'

Save the note on your device. Now, hold the amethyst crystal in the palm of your dominant hand and wait until it feels warm. When it's warm, place it near your device. Allow the candle to burn down safely.

You will find that your notifications and/or messages are few and far between now. When you're ready to re-enter the online world, go back into your notes app and delete the 'unavailable' note.

Gratitude Spell

PURPOSE

To express how thankful you feel

WHEN TO CAST

Any day and time during any moon phase

WHAT YOU NEED

a gold or yellow candle

a piece of paper

a gold pen

a glue stick

some gold glitter

a wand (see page 26)

When times get tough, it's more important than ever to practise gratitude for what you do have, even if it sometimes feels like you have nothing to be grateful for. It can be so easy to get consumed by the things that have gone wrong in your life, and to forget the things you have, such as having a roof over your head or food to eat. This gratitude spell helps to remind you of how blessed you really are, and it will put a new spring in your step. Perform this spell whenever you need a boost.

WHAT TO DO

Find a time when you can be alone for 30 minutes or so. Light your candle and sit down with your piece of paper and your gold pen. Think about everything you currently have to be grateful for. Begin with the simplest things, such as the air flowing in and out of your lungs, the blood moving around your body. Start writing them down.

Next concentrate on the material things you currently have in your life. This will be different for everyone. Do you have a car with fuel in it? Do you have a safe roof over your head? Do you have food in your cupboards? Are you able to go to work and earn your own money? Do you have water at the turn of a tap? Look around you at all the things you use and have access to without having to think about them. Do you have a phone, a computer, a watch, jewellery, sunglasses, a sofa to sit on, a Smart TV, access to the internet at the press of a button? These things you have are all things that you once didn't have and while it's easy to take them for granted, most of us would be lost without them, so we need to be grateful for every single item we have.

List as many things as you possibly can, because this is when the magic happens. Numerous studies have shown that when we are grateful for all we have, we attract more things to be grateful for. The problem is that we often become complacent and take the things we have for granted. We assume that we will wake up in the morning, and everything will be as it was. And so we rarely give thanks for what seems normal to us.

Once you feel happy with your list of things to be grateful for (and you might need several pages of paper once you get going), read through your list to remind yourself just how incredibly lucky you are. Next, take your glue stick and draw a big pentagram symbol in glue on the page or pages. Sprinkle your gold glitter all over the top, while visualizing glittery, positive energy jumping up out of the page and towards you.

Shake the excess glitter off the page and draw the outline of the pentagram with your wand over the paper. Say the following words:

I GIVE THANKS FOR ALL I HAVE.

I GIVE THANKS FOR ALL I AM.

I GIVE THANKS FOR ALL I WILL HAVE.

I GIVE THANKS FOR ALL I WILL BE.

BLESSED BE.

Allow your candle to burn down safely and keep your gratitude list somewhere safe so that you can refer to it next time you feel that life is getting tough. It's advisable to repeat this spell every three months; you'll be amazed at just how much your list increases each time.

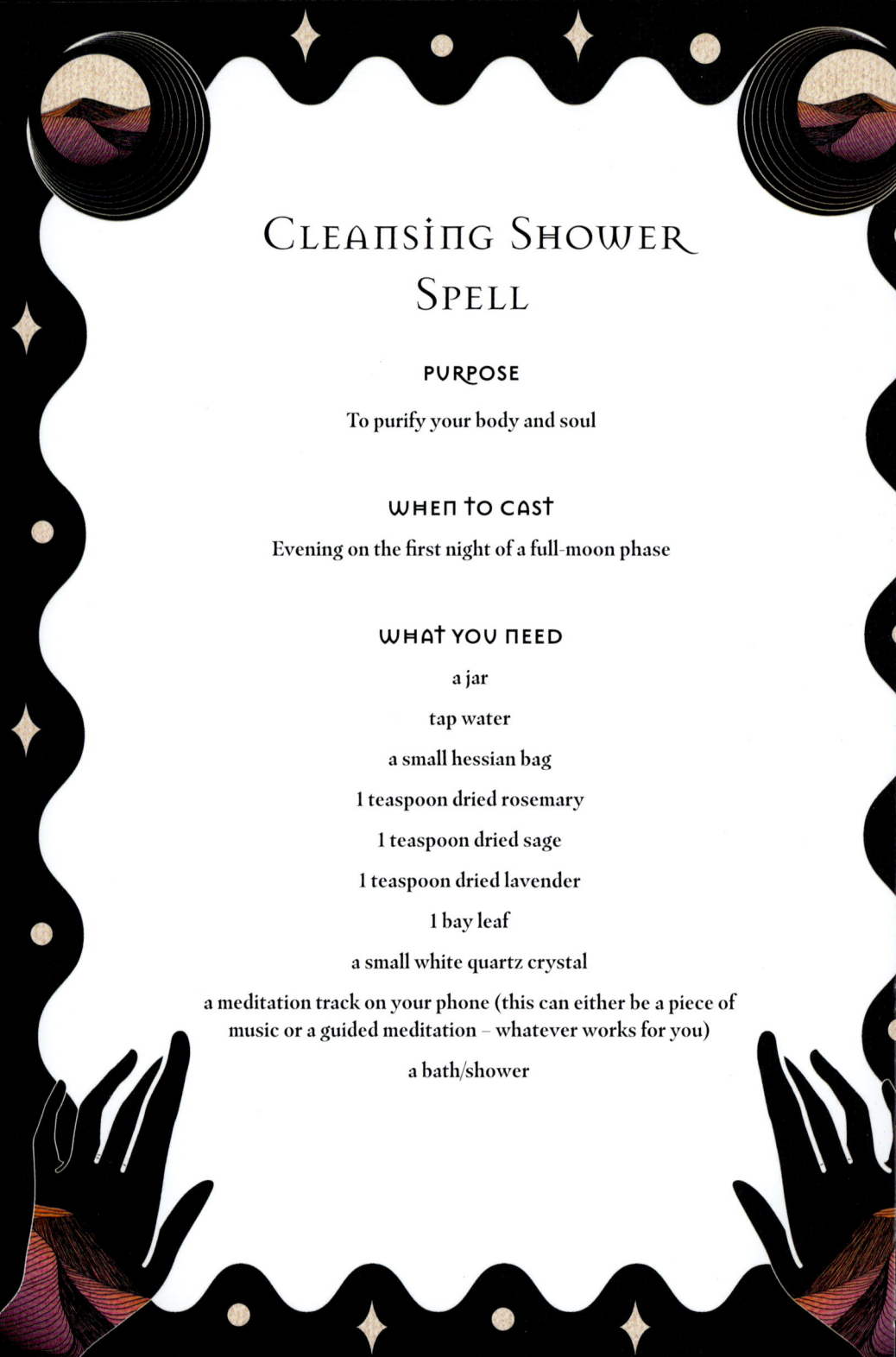

Cleansing Shower Spell

PURPOSE

To purify your body and soul

WHEN TO CAST

Evening on the first night of a full-moon phase

WHAT YOU NEED

a jar

tap water

a small hessian bag

1 teaspoon dried rosemary

1 teaspoon dried sage

1 teaspoon dried lavender

1 bay leaf

a small white quartz crystal

a meditation track on your phone (this can either be a piece of
music or a guided meditation – whatever works for you)

a bath/shower

Have you ever walked into a room, and it's just felt 'off', as though there's a bad presence there? Everything and everyone you encounter emits energy, and you absorb the energy that is around you – often without realizing it. If someone is having a karmic payback, their energy will reflect this. If you suddenly feel a bit off, or your mood changes suddenly, you could have picked up on someone else's negative energy, so you need to take a cleansing shower (or bath) to get rid of any negative energy that may have attached itself to you.

WHAT TO DO

On the first night of a full-moon phase, fill your jar with water and charge it outside under the light of the full moon.

The next day, carefully fill your hessian bag with the dried herbs and lavender, along with the bay leaf and your white quartz crystal. Tie the bag closed.

Get yourself ready for your shower or bath. Set up your phone or speaker to play your favourite mediation track and hang your cleansing hessian bag from either the taps on your bath, if using the bath method, or directly from your shower head if you're using the shower method.

Next, if you're using the bath, pour your moon water into the bath, or, if you're using your shower, step into the shower and pour the moon water over your head.

Visualize yourself washing away any negative energy that might have attached itself to you. Literally brush it off down your body as you wash yourself. Do this until the meditation track has finished. Watch as the water takes the negative energy with it and flows down the plughole. You can dispose of the bag in the bin.

You should now feel more like yourself and free of any negative energy. Repeat this as often as you like. In preparation for this and many other spells, I suggest you place a jar or bottle of water outside every full moon to make sure you always have moon water ready for future spells.

Karma Boost Spell

PURPOSE

To win yourself good karma points

WHEN TO CAST

Any day and time during any moon phase

WHAT YOU NEED

2 small sheets of paper (about 11 x 15cm/4½ x 6in)

a pen

a tall black candle

2 fireproof dishes

a tall silver candle

You wouldn't be human if you'd never made a mistake in your life, and all too often we beat ourselves up over something we've done or failed to do. It's very important to remember that we can't be 'good' all the time. Sometimes we do make unwise choices, and that's just life.

If you've been chastising yourself over something you feel wasn't a great decision, please don't worry, you're not destined to burn in hell! If, on the whole, you believe you are a good person, you will be fine – but just in case you are worrying, here is a good karma spell to use.

WHAT TO DO

Find some time when you can sit and write for 10 minutes. Take the first piece of paper and write down all the things you think you have done that could be considered 'bad' in some way. This could be something as simple as not responding to a text message or phone call, or something more serious such as cheating on your partner or losing your temper with someone close to you. Be honest with yourself, but remember: we all do things we're not proud of. It doesn't make you a bad person for the rest of your life, as long as you are able to recognize that what you did wasn't great and that you could have handled it better.

Once you have written down what's bothering you, light your black candle and say the following words as you burn the piece of paper with the flame of the candle:

By recognizing my bad deeds,
i release this feeling of back then.

i have learned my lessons,
i am now free to start again.

Drop the paper into the first fireproof dish and, once it has cooled, either bury the ashes in the ground away from your home or dispose of them in a rubbish bin outside your home. Allow the candle to burn down safely.

Now light the silver candle and, on the second piece of paper, write down all the good things that you have done lately, or are considering doing. This could be returning a message, phoning someone you haven't spoken to in ages, volunteering at a local shelter or paying for someone's coffee. It doesn't have to be anything extravagant. It's often the little things that people remember, like a kind smile or simply saying hello.

When you've finished writing, say the following words as you burn the piece of paper:

My karma is clean,
My karma is new,
From this day forth,
i bring to you
Nothing but goodness.

So mote it be.

Burn the second piece of paper and drop it into the second fireproof dish. When the ashes are cool, sprinkle them over a houseplant or a plant in your garden. Allow the silver candle to burn down safely. Your good karma will now be restored, and you will no longer feel guilty for any life blips you may have had.

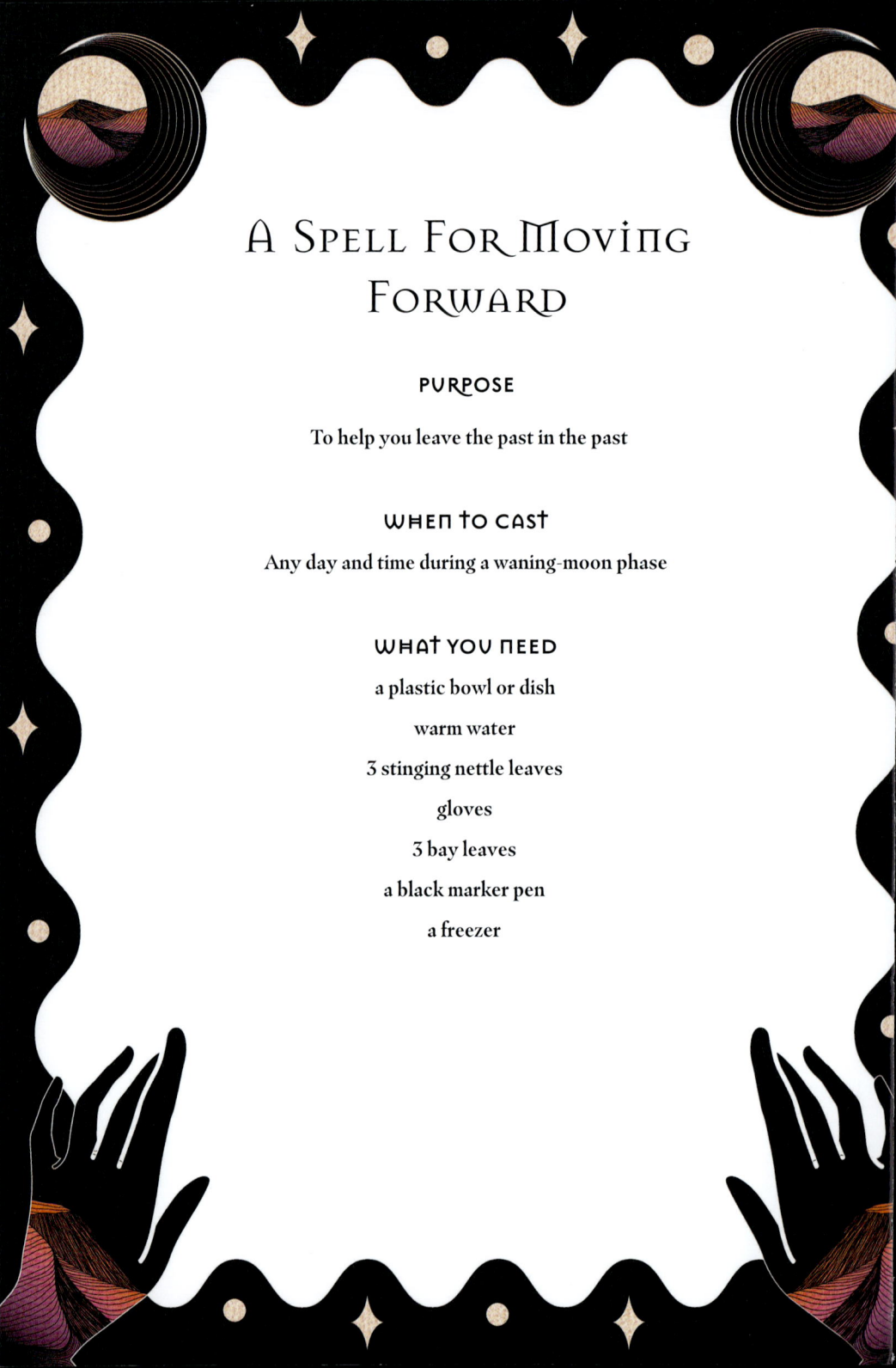

A Spell For Moving Forward

PURPOSE

To help you leave the past in the past

WHEN TO CAST

Any day and time during a waning-moon phase

WHAT YOU NEED

a plastic bowl or dish

warm water

3 stinging nettle leaves

gloves

3 bay leaves

a black marker pen

a freezer

Do you sometimes wish you could just rewind the not-so-pleasant parts of your life? This spell will help you to leave the past in the past and get on with your glorious new future.

WHAT TO DO

Magic is always about intention: the more intention you apply, the better your spells will work. For this spell to be successful, you need to fully intend that you will now lay the past to rest. There's a reason these things are in the past and not in your present or future, and there they should stay, regardless of how hurtful they might have been.

So, take as long as you like to bring up the thoughts and feelings that you want to bury in the past. This won't be easy, but it is necessary. If you need to get mad or sad, do so, but just for these few minutes.

Fill your bowl or dish with warm water, then pick three stinging nettle leaves (use gloves!) and place them into the water. Take one of the bay leaves, and on it, write the word 'BE' with your marker pen. On the second bay leaf, write the word 'GONE', and on the third leaf, write the word 'FOREVER'. Place the three bay leaves into the water bowl in order.

Imagine that all the pain, sadness and hurt from the past has now gone into the water. Take the bowl of water to the freezer and leave it to freeze for 24 hours. The following day, take the bowl of water (which should now be frozen) out of the freezer and carefully extract the frozen ice bowl from within the actual bowl, so that you have a bowl-shaped chunk of ice with bay leaves and nettles inside it. The ice crystals inside it should look jagged. This means the spell has worked.

Take your ice outside and either smash it on the ground until it breaks or leave it in a plant pot to melt away.

You can now forget about the past and move on with your fabulous life.

'Beautiful Me' Spell

PURPOSE

To bring back your confidence and own your appearance

WHEN TO CAST

Any day and time during any moon phase

WHAT YOU NEED

a cup of oats

3 teaspoons dried peppermint

a bowl and a spoon

a mashed banana

3 teaspoons natural yogurt

a squeeze of lemon juice

a mirror

red lipstick

We all have days when we feel more Shrek than princess, and it can have a huge effect on our mood and confidence. Always remember, you are a beautiful, unique soul, and beauty comes in all shapes, sizes and colours. If you're having a crisis of confidence or if someone has told you that you're not beautiful, cast this spell to remind yourself that you are indeed a beautiful human. Note: do not use this spell if you are allergic to any of the ingredients.

WHAT TO DO

You're going to make yourself a lovely facemask out of the listed ingredients, all of which have magical properties. Place the oats and peppermint in a bowl and mix together as you imagine the magic taking place. Next, add the mashed banana, natural yogurt and lemon juice, and mix to form a thick paste. Add more yogurt if it is too dry. Allow it to stand for a few minutes.

Pull your hair from your face and cover your shoulders with a towel, then spoon a handful of your magic facemask mix into your hands and rub it on to your face. It's important to remind yourself that you are beautiful inside and out, and that just because you don't adhere to stereotypes, it doesn't matter; you are as beautiful as any other human on this planet.

Relax for 10–20 minutes with your face covered in your magical facemask and keep reminding yourself of just how beautiful you are.

Rinse off the mixture and pat your face dry. Take your mirror (the bigger the better!) and, in red lipstick, write the words 'Beautiful Me' on the mirror. Every time you feel you're not beautiful, look in the mirror and read your note back to yourself.

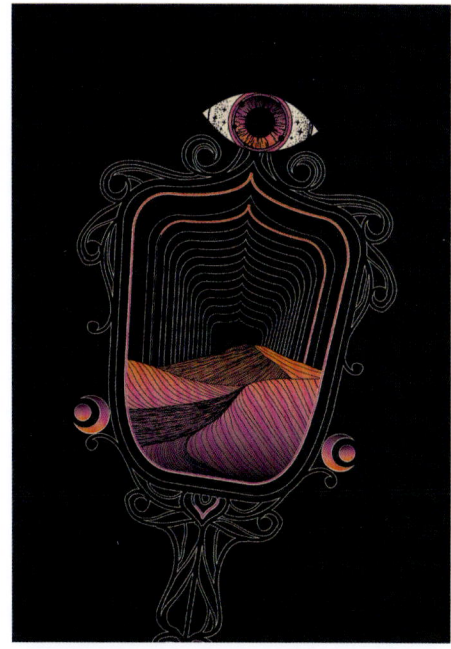

ABOUT THE AUTHOR

I'm Midia Star and I have been a solitary witch for over 40 years. I was introduced to all things spiritual, witchy and esoteric by my maternal grandmother, who was a medium, psychic and generally wise woman.

I was 15 when I became really interested in these mysteries and I began to learn all about Wicca and natural remedies. Since then, magic has been a way of life for me. I have written numerous books and hundreds of articles on the subject. Whether I've needed to increase my confidence, pass my driving test, or banish a harmful person from my life, witchcraft has always been there to help me, and I want it to be there for you, too.

My previous books include *There's a Little Witch in Every Woman*, *There's a Little Magic in Every Girl*, *There's a Little Prince in Every Frog*, *The Witchcraft Handbook* and *The Little Cauldron* series (all published by Octopus Publishing Group).

I wish you a fantastic magical journey into the world of witchcraft and spellcasting. Remember, you have the power within you to achieve everything you want in life. With a little sprinkle of magic, you will soon see just how powerful you really are.

Blessed be,
Midia Star x

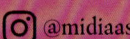 @midiaastar

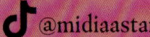 @midiaastar

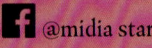 @midia star